IT HAPPENED TO ME

Series Editor: Arlene Hirschfelder

Books in the It Happened to Me series are designed for inquisitive teens digging for answers about certain illnesses, social issues, or lifestyle interests. Whether you are deep into your teen years or just entering them, these books are gold mines of up-to-date information, riveting teen views, and great visuals to help you figure out stuff. Besides special boxes highlighting singular facts, each book is enhanced with the latest reading lists, websites, and an index. Perfect for browsing, there are loads of expert information by acclaimed writers to help parents, guardians, and librarians understand teen illness, tough situations, and lifestyle choices.

DEPRESSION

THE ULTIMATE TEEN GUIDE

TINA P. SCHWARTZ

IT HAPPENED TO ME, NO. 42

ROWMAN & LITTLEFIELD
Lanham • Boulder • New York • London

Published by Rowman & Littlefield
A wholly owned subsidiary of The Rowman & Littlefield Publishing Group, Inc.
4501 Forbes Boulevard, Suite 200, Lanham, Maryland 20706
www.rowman.com

16 Carlisle Street, London W1D 3 BT, United Kingdom

British Library Cataloguing in Publication Information Available

Library of Congress Cataloging-in-Publication Data

Schwartz, Tina P., 1969–
   Depression : the ultimate teen guide / Tina P. Schwartz.
      pages cm. — (It happened to me)
   Includes bibliographical references and index.
   ISBN 978-0-8108-8387-1 (hardback : alk. paper) — ISBN 978-0-8108-8388-8 (ebook)
 1. Depression in adolescence—Popular works. I. Title.
   RJ506.D4S39 2014
   616.85'2700835—dc23   2014014437

∞™ The paper used in this publication meets the minimum requirements of American
National Standard for Information Sciences—Permanence of Paper for Printed Library
Materials, ANSI/NISO Z39.48-1992.

Printed in the United States of America

To Marc Schwartz, my beloved husband,
who loves me in dark times and light, and has never given up on me . . .
no matter what my mood. I love you with all my heart.—TS

Contents

Acknowledgments

To begin, I want to first and foremost thank my parents and siblings who helped me through the tough teen years with my own depression. My family was my lifeline through stormy waters. (Both my father, Jim Purcell, and my mother, Diane Purcell, died during the writing of this book, so I'd like to put in a special remembrance to them here. I loved them with all of my heart!) My husband and kids keep me happy and healthy today, and their constant encouragement of my work makes it a pleasure to keep on writing.

Next, I want to thank my editor, Arlene Hirschfelder, for her guidance (and editorial suggestions) during the writing of this book. She helped to shape it into something I am proud of. I'd also like to thank Debra Koenitz, LCPC, ATR-BC, who oversaw the technical content of the book and helped most with formulating the questionnaires for the teens who participated in the book. Her time, opinions, input, and edits are much appreciated.

A million thanks go to my critique partners Roger Peck, Lorijo Metz, and Anne Courtright, who catch any errors and question anything that's not quite right. Their critiques and coffee klatches keep the words flowing and red pen moving swiftly. I'd like to also thank Heather Schwartz, my daughter, for her beautiful photography, which adds an invaluable perspective to this book. I love you!

The biggest thanks go to the teen participants who were willing to share their stories, words, photography, and talents to make this book as authentic as possible. This book is for you!

I'd also like to thank John Baer for negotiating my contracts. I appreciate all you do for me.

Lastly, to the readers of this book, I appreciate you trusting me to tell the stories of the teens. I hope you find this helpful and encouraging, and know that you *will* get through this time in your lives. Although it may be difficult . . . never lose hope!

Disclaimer

The materials in this book are not meant to replace advice given by a medical doctor, counselor, or health-related professional. This is just a source of information and ideas to help readers cope with depression in its many forms.

Introduction

How do you describe a feeling of nothingness? Most people think of depression as sad
and crying all the time, but that's not the only way people with depression feel.
For me, it's a feeling of "who cares?" Work, parties, chores, homework—it's all so,
"blah . . ." I'd rather just sleep. I used to never sleep—it seemed, maybe 4 to 6 hours
a night, totally interrupted too, by wandering the house at night. Now I sleep all the
time and still can't get out of bed in the morning. I just feel nothing, like I can't be in
my own skin. Ya' know? I don't want to eat, or watch t.v., or talk on the phone, or
go on the Internet, or even take a shower. I can't sit still, yet I don't want to move,
to even breathe.—CGS, 20-something, journal entry[1]

It does not have to be that way. Feeling desperate or hopeless is no way to live. You *can* come through it. Depression has been called one of the most treatable illnesses. If you are depressed, you have an 80 percent chance of being helped.[2] However, nearly two out of three depressed people do not seek treatment for a variety of reasons.[3] The hardest thing to focus on is that things *can* get better. What you're feeling is temporary. Just hold on and seek the help you need! That's what my mother always told me, and you know what . . . she was right. Of course things go up and down, but nothing is forever—not sadness, not grief, not depression. Just because things don't work out how you want them to, doesn't mean they don't somehow work out in the end. This book is meant to encourage and enlighten teen readers with depression and those family and friends who love them.

Depression can become so all consuming that people who suffer from it can create tunnel vision and not even consider what their symptoms, behaviors, condition can do to those around them. It is important to remember that those closest to people with depression suffer from the effects of the condition, too. Their feelings should also be considered. Remember, you are not alone. It's like a popular e-mail that gets circulated on the web all the time:

1. There are at least two people in this world who would die for you.
2. At least fifteen people in this world love you in some way.
3. The only reason anyone would ever hate you is because they want to be just like you.

4. A smile from you can bring happiness to anyone, even if he or she doesn't like you.
5. Every night, SOMEONE thinks about you before he or she goes to sleep.
6. You mean the world to someone.
7. You are special and unique.
8. Someone you don't even know exists loves you.
9. When you make the biggest mistake ever, something good comes from it.
10. When you think the world has turned its back on you, take another look.
11. Always remember the compliments you received. Forget about the rude remarks.[4]

WARNING SIGNS AND SYMPTOMS

What Is Depression?

Almost one in six people will develop a major depression some time in his or her life. When people feel so low that they can't enjoy anything they used to, or even concentrate on everyday tasks, or if the depressed mood lasts for over two weeks, affects sleep, appetite, energy, or thoughts, then depression might be to blame.[1]

Depression is different from sadness or even grief. It can be based on biological factors or even stressful life events.[2] Things such as changing schools, divorce, or even a death in the family can trigger depression. The thing that differs from

Why can't I just feel normal?!

Major Depressive Episodes among Youth Ages 12–17[a]

Major Depressive Episode is defined as a period of at least two weeks when a person experiences a depressed mood or loss of interest or pleasure in daily activities plus at least five additional symptoms of depression (such as problems with sleep, eating, significant weight loss or gain, energy, concentration, feelings of self-worth, and recurrent thoughts of death (not just fear of dying) as described in the fifth edition of the *Diagnostic and Statistical Manual of Mental Disorders* (commonly referred to as the *DSM-5*).[b]

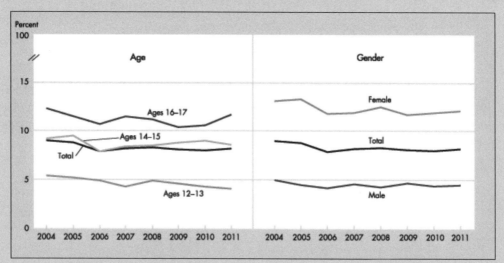

Indicator Health4: Percentage of youth ages 12–17 who experienced a major depressive episode (MDE) in the past year by age and gender, 2004–2011. *Federal Interagency Forum on Child and Family Statistics: America's Children: Key National Indicators of Well-Being, 2013.* Washington, DC: U.S. Government Printing Office.

person to person with depression can be the intensity, how long it lasts, and the symptoms a person deals with.[3]

Does Age Matter?

Depression in young people is similar to adults, however, not altogether identical. The way depression differs in young people is the way the symptoms present themselves.[4] To generalize, one might see a marked change in personality, doing poorly in school, or changing relationships with parents, friends, or boy- or girlfriend. Other signs include becoming tearful, appearing unhappy or down, complaining of emptiness, acting out aggressively, or losing interest in things previously enjoyed. Lastly, when teens isolate themselves, often staying in their rooms; have problems with concentration; have trouble organizing thoughts; and have an overall helpless or hopeless feeling about life's situations, depression might be to blame.

Before puberty, boys and girls are equally likely to develop depression. By age fifteen, however, girls are twice as likely as boys to have had a major depressive episode.

Depression during the teen years comes at a time of great personal change—when boys and girls are forming an identity apart from their parents, grappling with gender issues and emerging sexuality, and making independent decisions for the first time in their lives. Depression in adolescence frequently co-occurs with

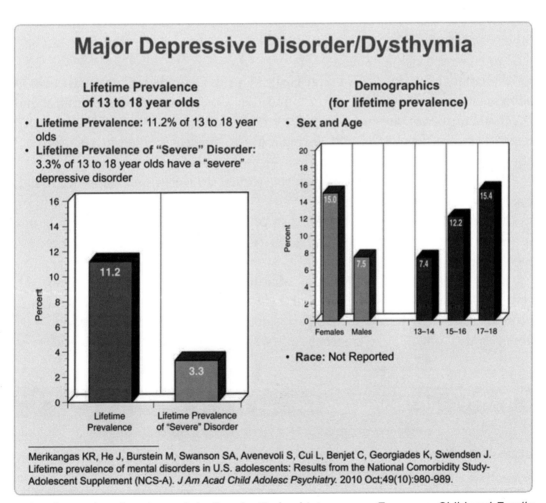

Merikangas KR, He J, Burstein M, Swanson SA, Avenevoli S, Cui L, Benjet C, Georgiades K, Swendsen J. Lifetime prevalence of mental disorders in U.S. adolescents: Results from the National Comorbidity Study-Adolescent Supplement (NCS-A). *J Am Acad Child Adolesc Psychiatry.* 2010 Oct;49(10):980-989.

Major depressive disorder and dysthymia. *Federal Interagency Forum on Child and Family Statistics: America's Children: Key National Indicators of Well-Being, 2013.* Washington, DC: U.S. Government Printing Office.

! Follow Your Gut Instinct

◉ When your friend (or your own child if you are a parent reading this) tells you to just "chill" or to "get off my back" but you feel in your heart that something is wrong, follow that instinct. You may feel you are pestering him or her or being overly cautious. However, your sixth sense might just be kicking in. Sometimes teens don't know how to ask for help, especially from friends. They might be embarrassed, or just be pretending that everything is fine, but you both know that it is a lie. Be careful not to do all the talking, too. Let *them* talk! If they won't talk to *you*, try to get them to confide in a teacher, parent, or even the school counselor or social worker. If you're not in school, go to a religious clergyman, or if it's of an immediate serious nature, you could even call 9-1-1.

other disorders such as anxiety, eating disorders, or substance abuse. It can also lead to increased risk for suicide.

A National Institute of Mental Health (NIMH)-funded clinical trial of 439 adolescents with major depression found that a combination of medication and psychotherapy was the most effective treatment option. Other NIMH-funded researchers are developing and testing ways to prevent suicide in children and adolescents.

Childhood depression often persists, recurs, and continues into adulthood, especially if left untreated.[5]

Major depressive disorder defined in previous image, differs from dysthymia in length of time experienced and severity. Dysthymia is often less severe, but more chronic, lasting for many months or even years.[6]

Many websites have checklists of what to look for in a depressed person. You can google "depression symptoms" and get a laundry list of symptoms similar to those mentioned on p. 5. The hard part is deciphering whether the person you care about is just "down," like a normal, everyday, emotion of feeling down/sad, or if

! Teenage Depression Test

◉ There is a teenage depression test known as the Kutcher Adolescent Depression Scale. You can take the test by going to www.aboutdepressionfacts .com/teenage-depression-test.html. While this isn't meant to replace a professional assessment, you can use it as a quick guide to see if, perhaps, you need to investigate your symptoms further.

he or she may be truly "clinically depressed." To differentiate between the two, look at the length of time the symptoms last. Sadness lasts for a few days or happens occasionally. Clinical depression goes on for more than two weeks and affects one's ability to function at home, work, or with family, friends, or colleagues.[7]

How Is Clinical Depression Diagnosed?

The following table should help you differentiate between the two, regular sadness and clinical depression.

Sadness	*Clinical Depression*
1. Tired a lot	1. Sleeping many more hours than usual
2. Mild insomnia	2. Insomnia that lasts more than a few days
3. Occasionally skipping showers	3. Constantly having dirty hair, disheveled clothes, and poor hygiene or self-care
4. Feeling a bit weepy, especially after a loss or change	4. Uncontrollable crying, or crying several times a week without knowing why
5. Mildly losing interest in things you once enjoyed	5. Quitting a sports team or completely cutting off ties with activities altogether
6. Feeling uneasy once in a while	6. Feeling frequent anxiety or worry and not quite right in your own skin
7. Occasional overeating	7. Binge eating where you feel out of control, or constant late-night snacking
8. Decreased appetite	8. Unable to make yourself eat or "forgetting to eat" frequently

If you're still not sure that you, or your loved one, are clinically depressed, there are assessments that a doctor can perform to help make a diagnosis. Some of these screening tests are called HAM-D, or Hamilton Depression Scale; CDI, or Child Depression Inventory; BDI, or Beck Depression Inventory; and the Zung Self-Rating Scale for Depression. You can ask your general family practitioner (doctor), psychiatrist, or a therapist (social worker, counselor, or psychologist) if he or she is familiar with any of these assessment tests.

I Know My Friend Is Depressed, So What Can I Do to Help?

The first thing you can do for someone who is depressed, or whom you suspect may be depressed, is offer support—let the person know you are there for her.

German Test Regarding "Specificity" and "Sensitivity" to Diagnose Depression in Teens

In 2012, Kathrin Pietsch, from Ludwig-Maximilians University in Munich, headed a German research team searching for a solution to correctly diagnose depression in adolescents. Their goal was actively testing the teenage population for depression. According to an article in *Child and Adolescent Mental Health*, doctors correctly recognize fewer than 30 percent of the depressive cases in front of them. For the other 70 percent who were undiagnosed, there was an increased likelihood of suicide. Obviously, another way of detecting depression is needed.

According to Pietsch, the solution is screening—actively testing the teenage population for the disorder of depression. She felt that it depended highly on the questionnaires used for screening, and most important were two specific characteristics. First, a good screener needs to be easy to use, not adding much work for those administering it. So it should be kept short. Second, it should be both sensitive and specific. That is, it needs to be good at discriminating between those who have depression and those who don't. *Sensitivity* relates to the number of cases correctly identified (those who actually have depression).

Pietsch's team chose a short fifteen-item version of the Center for Epidemiological Studies Depression Scale (CES-D). This shortened version of the scale was quick and easy to complete and was shown to measure adolescent depression more accurately, although it had not been used to identify clinical cases of depression.

This is where Pietsch and colleagues' study began. The research team looked to find the best threshold score on the CES-D for identifying those adolescents with depression. The team asked 332 thirteen- to sixteen-year-olds staying in a hospital to complete the CES-D. The teens also underwent a structured diagnostic interview, which is what is widely used for detecting depression. Pietsch's team reviewed results of the participants' interview versus the CES-D, examining the sensitivity and specificity of several different threshold scores. As the specificity of a measure goes up, its sensitivity goes down. Therefore, it was important that the research team find a compromise between correctly identifying all cases of depression and ensuring that those defined as depressed were in fact depressed. High sensitivity is especially crucial for a good screening instrument, since the main purpose is to identify a high proportion of likely depressed teens ahead of further assessment.

Based on this premise, Pietsch and colleagues concluded that a score of 14 on the CES-D would lead to the highest level of sensitivity without sacrificing so much specificity as to render the CES-D useless. The idea is that it would then flag 85 percent of the true cases of depression and correctly recognize the absence of depression in 84 percent of the nondepressed teens.[c]

As you can see, the importance of recognizing the absence of depression can be just as important to a study as finding true cases of depression.

Then, be gentle but persistent in getting her to talk about what feelings she is having. It's tough and scary for a person to admit to himself, let alone another friend or family member, that he is feeling depressed. Another thing to remember is to listen without lecturing. If you criticize someone or pass judgment (e.g., "You have such a great life! You couldn't possibly be depressed with all you have going for you."), that doesn't help anybody at all! Lastly, validate her feelings, even if the feelings seem irrational to you. Acknowledge the pain and sadness the depressed person is feeling, or she won't trust or confide in you anymore, especially if she feels you are not taking her emotions seriously.[8]

The Numbers: How Many Teens Get Depressed?

According to a 2004 study by the National Survey on Drug Use and Health, 10 percent of kids between the ages of twelve and seventeen have had at least one major depressive episode.[9] The proportion is equal for guys and girls until adolescence, then the numbers jump to girls having twice as much of a chance of suffering from depression from the teens years into adulthood.[10]

According to Gabriel Cousens, MD, and Mark Mayell in their book *Depression-Free for Life: An All-Natural, 5-Step Plan to Reclaim Your Zest for Living*, doctors estimate that as many as 8 million women and 4 million men are treated for clinical depression each year in the United States. The book goes on to report that an estimated 12 million people suffer from depression without realizing it![11]

Blood Test to Diagnose Depression in Teens?

Time.com published an online article April 17, 2012, by Alexandra Sifferlin, that talked about a possible blood test being developed to diagnose teen depression. While it is still in the early stages, the idea could help in myriad ways. Not only would it help make an earlier diagnosis, permitting teens to get help sooner, but it would also help suggest that mental illness has biological origins. This would lessen the stigma and would bring it into the open.

Eva Redei, a professor of psychiatry and behavioral sciences at Northwestern University Feinberg School of Medicine, ran the test. She and her team conducted a study about depression in teens at the Research Institute of Nationwide Children's Hospital in Columbus, Ohio. They studied fourteen teens with major depression and fourteen nondepressed teens, ages fifteen to nineteen. While the investigation was very small, initially, it was based on years of research done on rats. However, more extensive research will be needed to make the findings conclusive. While it is too early to consider the problem of diagnosing teen depression solved, it is an exciting step toward that conclusion.

In the study, teens' blood was tested for twenty-six genetic markers of major depression. Eleven markers showed up in depressed teens but not in healthy teens. In addition, eighteen of the markers were able to show teens with depression only or teens with depression and other anxiety disorders.

Although this study is in the early stages, it is an exciting breakthrough for those who suffer in silence. It validates that mental illness has biological origins just like any other disease.[d]

Recognizing Depression in Children and Teens

It may be hard for parents to see if you as a teen—or even a child—are depressed. Since they are with you on a day-to-day basis, noticing gradual changes may not be as easy to detect as you might think. It is often a family friend who might notice the changes right away. Your parents might detect your depression if they notice

"I never told any adults how I was feeling [depressed]. . . . I thought adults would treat my problem like it was nothing because I was so young. I started feeling depressed in the sixth grade."

"When I'm depressed I just want to cry a lot, but then I get to thinking that I have no right to be crying because there are people worse off than me, but I just can't help it. I try to convince myself that it is going to get better from that point on, but that just makes it worse because my brain is convinced that it is not. When I'm depressed, I feel like I don't belong—anywhere!"
—Kathryn, age 14[e]

you are extra crabby and snap at them more often than usual, if you are more sensitive than you normally might be, or if you are withdrawn—often isolating yourself in your room or being seemingly lazy, that is, you don't want to do anything that brought you enjoyment in the past. Getting you to open up about your feelings can help diagnose if you are indeed depressed.

Variety of Sleep Issues

There are several sleep issues associated with depression. One is insomnia, or the inability to fall asleep. This is more typical for anxiety, not necessarily depression, but depression could be the cause. However, there are other sleep disorders to be aware of:

- Early morning rising, or terminal insomnia—where a person wakes up too early (approximately two or more hours before they need to rise) and can't fall back asleep.
- Middle insomnia—waking up after being asleep, but for no apparent reason (such as going to the bathroom, nightmare, etc.).
- Middle awakening dream carryover—person wakes from a dream but doesn't realize it was just a dream for over ten seconds. (This can be a symptom of depression with psychosis.)
- Nightmares—can be from depression, anxiety, or some other medical problems. The side effects are sweating, shaking, or palpitations.
- Reversed sleep patterns—people who suffer from this have very poor sleep at night, therefore needing to nap during the day. This is commonly

"I have a hard time sleeping at night and a hard time waking up in the morning. I tend to want to nap a lot when I'm at the heights of a 'depressed mood.'"—Veronica, early 20s[f]

a symptom of depression. (*The exception to this symptom and depression is, of course, people who work the night shift, or third shift, at a company.*)[12]

Males versus Females

Women are twice as likely as men to report (or admit to) depression.[13] Young girls appear to be more susceptible to depression than boys. In fact, although both go through puberty at somewhat the same time, adolescent girls develop depressive symptoms at an earlier age than do adolescent boys. There's no concrete evidence to prove why.[14]

For girls, puberty often happens during middle school, which is a difficult transition period in one's life already.[15] Oftentimes boys go through puberty later, after the rough transition to middle school. Therefore, by the time boys go through puberty, their self-image and confidence have had a chance to develop positively.

Teen girls have been noted to cope differently than teen boys.[16] By internalizing things such as rejection, broken relationships, and negative body image, they are more vulnerable to depression. Feeling different in something as huge as going through puberty—for example, being one of the first to menstruate—can add to the feelings of low self-worth and lower one's self-esteem.

In 2003, in a study done in central Iowa, 451 families were interviewed over a six-year period.[17] The results from that study showed initial depressive symptoms found in early adolescence carried over into the mid to late teens. Considering both biological factors and stress, girls carried a greater risk for depression than boys. Starting when girls are as young as twelve years of age, there are consistent gender differences from that age on. This was the first study to ever report such findings.[18]

On the National Institute of Mental Health's government website, there is more evidence about the difference in boys and girls being affected by depression throughout adolescence.[19] It states that *before* the teen years, girls and boys experience depression at approximately the same rate. However, by the time puberty occurs there is a sharp increase in depression rates for girls. The site says that compared to boys, girls tend to need more approval and success to feel secure. Lastly, girls tend to doubt themselves and their problem-solving abilities and view their problems as "unsolvable" more often than boys do, according to a 2005 study by Calvete and Cardenoso in the *Journal of Abnormal Child Psychology*.[20]

In her book *The Disappearing Girl*, Dr. Lisa Machoian discusses the difficulties girls face when changing from a smaller school to a larger one, such as middle school to high school. It seems that just when they (girls) have figured out the culture, cliques, and groups of middle school, and the different ways of teachers, they have to move up to high school and start all over again. Some girls have difficulty with the disruption of friendships and ordinary routines like studying, making transitions a time of heightened risk for some girls.[21]

Here are some helpful hints for parents to alleviate the potential troubling times for any teen:

- Make sure he is enrolled in some sort of regular/consistent physical activity; endorphins will help with improving mood.
- Allow her to find a peer group to interact with. If you're going to a family function, you might consider letting her bring a friend along.
- Regular spiritual or religious affiliations have been known to show a positive influence on a person. It can be a source of hopefulness and belonging.
- Allow your teen to help others by volunteering somewhere like a shelter, a soup kitchen, or even an after-school tutoring program at school. Helping others can help take the focus off someone's own problems, and shift focus onto a new or distracting subject for a while. It can help a teen "get out of her own head," so to speak.
- Spend time simply in the same room as your teen. Even if you're reading a book and he is texting a friend, occasionally he will stop and feel your

What Other Diseases Can Trigger Depression, and How Debilitating Is Such a Mental Disorder?

According to the National Institute of Mental Health (NIMH), people with heart disease, cancer, HIV/AIDS, or diabetes may also have depression at the same time. When the two coexist, there can be more severe symptoms of depression and the physical illness, plus a more difficult time adjusting to the physical condition.[9]

The American Psychiatric Association (APA) reported international and national findings regarding mental disorders. The APA said that "according to a landmark study by the World Health Organization, the World Bank, and Harvard University, mental disorders are so disabling that, in established market economies like the United States, they rank second only to cardiovascular disease in their impact on disability."[h]

presence and oftentimes begin a conversation. This comes out organically and not forced because you are simply interacting naturally.

Paying for Care

When you're a teen, you shouldn't have to worry about how you're going to pay for being treated for depression, but here's information for you and your parents to help put your (and their) mind at ease. To begin, a doctor may very likely put you on an antidepressant, which will be discussed in a later chapter. These medications, antidepressants, even in generic form can be very expensive. The first thing you can do is ask for free samples from your doctor. He or she might be able to give you enough for a few weeks, which might be enough time to see if a particular drug is effective in treating your depression.

Since you can't rely on free samples forever, the next place to look for help is *patient assistant programs*. These programs are offered by drug companies to people who don't have insurance or don't have a drug benefit in their plans.[22] Most doctors are not familiar with the various programs offered, so you'd do best by going on the Internet to do some research. Your parents will have to fill out paperwork showing the financial need for such a program, proof of or lack of insurance, among other details. Your doctor may need to fill out some paperwork on your behalf, as well. It can be very tedious but worthwhile in the end, saving you much money over the course of your treatment. For further information, check out some of these websites to learn more:

Free Medicine Foundation, www.freemedicinefoundation.com, 1-573-996-3333
The Medicine Program, www.themedicineprogram.com
Partnership for Prescription Assistance, www.pparx.org, 1-888-477-2669
RxOutreach, www.rxassist.org

EXTERNAL (OR SITUATIONAL) TRIGGERS OF YOUR DEPRESSION

··

While some depression is hereditary, a chemical imbalance in the brain, depression can also be triggered by external factors such as bullying, witnessing a violent crime, loss of a loved one, ending of a relationship, leaving home for the first time to go to college, the military, or even getting your first apartment. This chapter will touch on many of the external triggers, while biochemical reasons will be covered in the next chapter. (Healthy coping mechanisms will be discussed in a later chapter, as well.)

Post-Traumatic Stress Disorder

Post-traumatic stress disorder (PTSD) is a disorder of circumstance, really. Symptoms following exposure to an extremely traumatic event that involves actual or threatened death, serious injury, or sexual violence in one or more of the following ways listed in the *DSM-5* (*Diagnostic and Statistical Manual of Mental Disorders*) are part of what categorize PTSD.[1] This is a serious disorder that one should seek counseling for to get through and process, and medication might be recommended as well. PTSD can make your depression flare up.

PTSD in children and teens has not been as extensively researched in comparison to its presence in adults. There are different therapies that can help with PTSD in kids and teens, including the following:

- *Cognitive behavioral therapy (CBT)*—This type of therapy teaches a person to retrain his thinking so he doesn't necessarily assume the worst possible outcome will happen from a single event.

Try to notice things that may be "external triggers" of your depression, and eliminate them whenever possible.

CBT benefits children and teens because they can see their trauma from a different perspective, from another person's point of view besides their own. The therapy can increase their confidence by lessening their fears and distress, which may begin to fade away. A therapist is a person who can help a child or teen realize that not all bad things will end in disaster. For example, if a parent gets into a car accident, it doesn't necessarily mean it will be a fatal accident. A therapist can help a child or teen feel less fearful of crises that might arise in the future.[2]

- *Eye movement desensitization and reprocessing therapy*—This is a therapy in which a teen (or child) follows a therapist's finger, with her eyes, as the therapist moves his finger slowly and steadily from side to side while the patient recalls the trauma in small segments. (The same approach is used for adults. However, children often react quicker to therapy and therefore require fewer sessions.)[3]

- *Play therapy*—This is often used on children younger than teens. It is mentioned in case you have ever gone through such therapy, or have heard of it, due to a trauma experienced when you were younger. Since young children sometimes have one-tenth the vocabulary of an adult, they have

"Stress is a part of normal physical response to events that make you feel threatened or upset. It's also the body's way of rising to a challenge and preparing to meet a tough situation. Stress can either be good or bad, but there are many different types and causes of stress. The effects of stress can be short or long term, and can hurt a person physically or mentally. "The consequences of stress can lead to depression, anxiety, and addictive disorders."—Stephanie, teen writer featured in *TeenInk.com*[a]

a harder time expressing themselves verbally. By using play therapy they can act out occurrences or feelings with dolls, cars, sand, crayons, and so on. A therapist can watch how a child plays to ask questions about the feelings the boy or girl may be experiencing. This can be helpful for older children, too, who have trouble speaking about their traumas.[4]

- *Medications*—Turning to medication is a difficult decision to make when dealing with a child or teen. The reason is that young bodies are still growing and changing, biologically. Their brain functions and metabolism are developing; therefore, it is always wise to research medication extensively and have it monitored very carefully by a doctor. The biggest risk of younger people taking medications such as antidepressants is that of suicidal thoughts and behaviors. Lastly, if it is decided that medication is the best choice, it should be teamed with psychological therapy as well to get the greatest benefits.[5] (See more information on medications in chapter 11.)

- *Exposure therapy*—The goal of this type of therapy is to talk about a trauma over and over again, to desensitize oneself from the event(s). Ideally, the person will learn not to be afraid of his memories, and to feel less upset when dealing with the process of recalling them. When someone has a particularly stressful time or trigger of a memory, he can also revert to breathing techniques, discussed in chapter 10, to ease anxiety.[6]

Bullying

Physical and emotional bullying is all too commonplace in America these days. It has become so rampant that schools are holding seminars on antibullying and creating a zero-tolerance policy for the act. If you're being abused through bullying, it is important to tell someone about it. Bullying can start out with something as seemingly small as a snide comment, to passing notes, to de-friending you on Facebook. But it can quickly escalate to more serious actions such as posting

Adoption

If you are adopted, when did you learn that fact? Did you know for as long as you can remember, or were you told in some way at an age that you can remember? At some point many adoptees have a "curiosity," for lack of a better term, for *why* they were put up for adoption . . . what was the *story*?

No matter how great the story of your real parents adopting you is (e.g., "We waited and prayed for a miracle, and you were born!"), the feelings of loss over being given up for adoption may weigh heavily on you from time to time. The uncertainty of feeling rejected, whether real or imagined, can toy with your emotional well-being if not addressed.

Finding out about your adoption can be an emotional trigger for depression. If it was told to you later in life, you might question all that you've known up to the present. What you've known as your "world" can feel turned upside down, and that can be upsetting. Find out what you need to in order to satisfy your questions about your life and your personal journey. You may or may not have questions about your birth parents, and even about your real parents . . . the ones who have raised you. Having an open and honest discussion in which you can ask questions can be very helpful to calming your fears and worries. Seeking counseling yourself, or as a family, is often a helpful option.

slanderous statements or unacceptable photos on the Internet to physical abuse. If you are feeling bullied, this can definitely trigger a depression. You need to reach out for help to make the abuse stop! (See more about bullying in chapter 5.)

Divorce or a Parent Who Leaves

When a parent abandons a child or the whole family, severe trauma ensues. Feelings of loss, helplessness, and depression often follow. Sometimes, there is a divorce where both parents are still present, but the child(ren) must be split between houses. This upheaval of the family dynamic can cause upsetting feelings and even depression. The feelings of abandonment must be addressed so they don't cause hurdles later in life with future relationships. Often a family will go through counseling to handle the new family unit postdivorce or separation. If your family doesn't go through counseling, there are support groups and many books on how to process the devastation of divorce.

When a family is divided by a divorce that is not amicable, teens and children often feel as though they have to "choose sides." This is a horrible position to be placed in! Your loyalty to one parent or another can be tested, and that is a huge burden for anyone to face, especially someone so young. If you add stepparents, stepsiblings, or even half-siblings into the family mix, it can open up a whole new set of adjustments for you. Finding an adult to speak with is important. If you don't feel comfortable seeking out an adult, perhaps you can find another teen who is dealing with a similar situation. What did he do to get through it? Who did she talk to? Did the teen attend a peer support group and how did he find it? These are important questions to have answered.

If, in an extreme case, there is a danger of one parent or the other kidnapping you, please seek out an authority figure! Whether it be a counselor at school, or a grandparent, or some other adult, even 9-1-1, don't try to face such obstacles on your own.

Disruptive Home Life

Sometimes parents stay together "for the sake of the children." This is not always the healthiest choice for a family or the children involved. Sometimes children witnessing arguments, verbal and/or physical, can do more harm than good.

Sometimes it can be another family member who is upsetting the home atmosphere. Perhaps you have a sibling who is troubled. Has he been kicked out of school, or maybe even arrested? Perhaps he is abusing drugs or alcohol, and it's taking its toll on the family's well-being. This is another way that your home life might not be the safe and warm environment you are wishing for. If you're dealing with a disruptive home life, it could be an external or situational trigger for your depression.

Moving

Whether you have to move from a house to an apartment in the same town, or move from one home to another in a different state, this can be a trigger for depression. Having to switch neighborhoods or even schools can change your entire world. You might not know anyone in your new town, and you will have to make new friends. This is one of the biggest adjustments that can happen in anyone's life. But it is especially difficult in the teen years. Perhaps you've grown up in one

> "My depression started when I was seven years old. My best friend was deported back to Japan. I remember missing her so much but no one understood me. They all thought I was too young to feel such pain so they would tell me I'd get over it. It was my first loss. I kept journals since I was that age and I would write about missing her and I how I felt 'different' in some way. I said I liked that I was different, but I felt no one would ever understand me. I felt I would never be able to connect to another human being."—Susan, age 20[b]

town, having the same friends throughout all of grade school. Now that you're in high school, being uprooted from your surroundings and all that you've ever known might be traumatic for you. If possible, try to take part in some teen activities in your new hometown such as park district sports, or a writing group at the library, or even some sort of community theater or musical group. If you can lay a foundation for meeting new peers before you have to go to school, it will help you to find a friendly face in the crowd while you navigate your way around a whole new atmosphere.

Perhaps you've graduated high school and have opted not to continue on to college. You're ready for the workforce and decide to get your first apartment. That's exciting! Techniques such as CBT, described earlier, will help you take this transition one step at a time and help you not feel overwhelmed or afraid of what your future holds. Things don't always go wrong in life; many times, they go great!

Love Lost: Friend

As an adult, I know from experience that not all friendships last forever. There's a saying that goes "friend for a reason, for a season, for a lifetime." What this means is that sometimes friends are there to help us through a tough time ("a reason"); then after the trauma, the friendship kind of just fades away. "Friend for a season" can mean a time in life, like middle school or high school, and the friendship might simply dissolve, or you might grow apart, or there might even be a falling out. "Friend for a lifetime" is just that—someone who is with you for many of the milestones in your life. Perhaps you met him in grade school, continued your friendship through middle and high schools, and even went on to college together. This could be a friend whose wedding you stand up in one day,

"During senior year of college, my roommate and I were having problems with her boyfriend hitting on me. I assured her I had no interest and would never do anything to harm our friendship. She was cheating on him, and he on her, so I tried to stay far out of their relationship troubles.

"After one fight we girls had with each other, I wrote her a letter, venting all of my frustrations about her insecurities and (what I thought of as) bad behaviors. She was furious and threw all of my belongings out of the house we were renting. She never spoke to me again, and that was a few years ago. She was my best friend, and I was so distraught, I finally went to a counselor to try and talk out my feelings. It's been a few years, and the couple are no longer together, and I'm not friends with either one anymore. It was a devastating situation that still stings to this day. I'm grateful to the counselor I see for helping me learn to accept that this friendship will probably never reconnect, but that still makes me very sad."
—CGS, 20-something[c]

whose child you will spoil, whose hand you will hold through losing grandparents, parents, and so on.

When a friendship ends, this can be traumatic. Having a friend whom you talk to regularly is something you can depend on. When that is gone, it can trigger a feeling of loss, or a depression. Sometimes friendships dissolve and fade away, other times there are problems or a big fight that causes a break in the relationship. Losing someone you have constant contact with can really make a change in your life, and the feelings of loss can be devastating. There are self-help books, websites, and articles on the subject. You may even want to seek therapy to help get you through the loss.

Love Lost: Romantically

Breakups are never easy as an adult or as a young adult. Loss at any age is difficult to accept. Whether you are the one to do the breaking up or are broken up with, a grieving process must take place. It is important not to let the grief overcome you and make you spiral down into a deep depression. You cannot let it make your life

"I met my boyfriend in high school driver's ed. We were fifteen years old. We dated for a year and broke up. Then we got back together a year later, the summer before senior year of high school, and dated all the way through senior year of college. We went to school six hours apart, but tried our best to make it work. We talked about getting engaged right after graduation, and it was exciting. I had dated him from age fifteen to age twenty-one, essentially. I was afraid his drinking was getting in the way, though, and ultimately decided I couldn't start a life with such a huge hurdle, as I had seen alcoholism in my family and knew the damage it could do if untreated. (I'm not sure if he was an alcoholic, but I knew he was a problem drinker for sure!) I finally ended the relationship, but was so sad and consumed. I guess you could say I went into a deep depression. I was seeing a counselor at the time, so he helped me work through it. I made the right decision, but it definitely wasn't the easy decision. If you are in a tough situation, sometimes you have to make a horrible decision to cut ties. That's what I did. I don't regret it, but I still think of him often."—CGS, 20-something[d]

feel over. Even if it was an all-consuming relationship, remember, you will have other relationships throughout your life. You have to trust in that. Sometimes relationships just end.

By focusing on other aspects of your life, you can let your heart heal. While the trite saying "Time heals all wounds" isn't particularly helpful at the time, there is some truth to the sentiment. Giving your mind, body, and spirit time to heal and get over the loss can be what is needed. Sometimes, you might want to seek the help of a professional counselor. Having someone, more specifically a professional, to talk to about your feelings can help you process the loss. There are support groups that you might find helpful as well, if you are uncomfortable seeking out one-on-one counseling.

Love Lost: Death of a Pet

Pets are some of the most underrated creatures on earth. People who don't have them don't understand how much they impact one's life. Losing a pet can be very traumatic. It's like losing a family member. If you've recently lost your pet to death or running away, this could aggravate your depression and its symptoms. You need to give yourself permission to grieve and go through the process of losing someone you love. There are books on how to help deal with this loss, including one in the It Happened to Me series titled *Animals and Teens: The Ultimate Teen Guide*, by Gail Green (2009). Just know that you are not alone in your grief, and it is a real loss when a pet dies.

Leaving Home for the First Time: College, Camp, Study Abroad, Military

While going away to college can be an exciting time for teens—the thought of having their own place without curfews or adults to answer to—it can be a time of great stress and even depression. After years of planning and working in high school for great grades, athletics, social clubs, part-time jobs, and other extracurricular activities to put on college applications to stand out from the crowd, you might feel emotional after so much effort has gone into the process. For some, the adrenalin can be a high while going on school visits and sending out multiple applications; then when it is all finally over and decisions have been made, there can be a natural let down.

Stresses about being away at college can come in many forms. It can start with separation from parents for the first time in a person's life. Then money might be an issue, from signing college loans, to finding a job while at school, to balancing studies with work. Also, there is the stress of having to make a whole new group of friends among a sea of strangers.

College professors usually expect more from students than high school teachers. However, there isn't always the pressure from professors to do well. After all, students can go to class or not go to class without consequence. It is up to the student to show up, study, and do well. Professors don't have time to "babysit" students, whereas in high school, if a student skipped class, she would get a detention or a note home. In college, no one really cares if you attend class. This places a lot of pressure on a student to act as an adult and impose rules and regulations on himself. Without an adult to nudge or suggest good study habits, being responsible for self-discipline can be a huge undertaking for a teen on her own for the first time in life. This can be more pressure than the student expected. Oftentimes, teens fail because of this. Some lack the direction or guidance necessary to succeed.

Lastly the pressure to have things all figured out can be too great for teens, whether they go to college or enter the workforce right after high school. They are expected to know what they want to be when they grow up. Adults realize you can change your major area of study in college many times, but as a teen things feel so final and in concrete. As a teen, you may not realize that you can undo decisions you've made by changing majors or changing schools, for example. This can be a great source of tension and even lead to depression.

Perhaps you're going away from home for the first time to attend a summer camp or even to study abroad. Although you are only leaving home temporarily, this can cause mixed feelings or anxiety or even lead to a depression. You need to focus on the experiences you'll be having and try to enjoy your time away.

Perhaps you've made a larger decision. Instead of simply studying abroad temporarily, you've decided to make a choice that lasts many years, such as going into the military. This decision is huge and can be a life-changing decision, so it may come with a myriad of emotions. You're making an important, adult decision about your future. First, take a deep breath and congratulate yourself on such a large achievement. This life choice will affect many people, some of whom you don't even know. But don't let that weigh heavily on your mind. Think of the positive aspects of your decision. It will transition you into adulthood, and joining the military will become a career you can take pride in. You will learn so many life skills!

Problems at School

If you are doing poorly at school, that doesn't mean you are necessarily going to fail out. It may not be too late to reach out for help. You can go to a teacher for extra credit, or ask your parents about getting you a tutor to help you with your difficult subjects. It is not hopeless.

Say things are past the point of no return with your grades, and you find that you are going to fail out of high school or college. This possibility could be enough of an issue to trigger a depression. This may or may not lead to clinical depression but could certainly amount to a serious traumatic event.

But as with all of life's struggles, failure can often lead to success. Perhaps the school, or even the major area of study you chose, just wasn't right for you. There are so many choices and options in life; another idea could come up and be even more suited to your needs and desires. If the high school atmosphere was overwhelming or you had other obstacles such as bullying to contend with, you could choose to get your GED instead. You can still finish school that way. If you are older and college was too much to handle, being away from home for the first time, perhaps you can come back and go to a community college for the first couple of years until you are ready to try moving away again.

I have a friend who desperately wanted to be a pilot. It was his goal throughout adolescence. When it came time to decide on a major for college, he was distraught to find out that he was color-blind. The fact is that you cannot be a pilot if you are color-blind. It wasn't something he could change; he just had to accept that and make alternate plans. He had a depressive episode at the time, and while he felt a huge loss and fear of the unknown, he ended up picking a totally different major and excelling at it. He became a successful commodities trader.

Sometimes taking a step back and reevaluating your life isn't always a horrible thing. It might *feel* horrible and scary, but this reevaluation can put you on a different and better life path.

It is important to seek help with getting your life back on track. Let's say again that you're failing out of high school; that is a problem you will need help correcting. Getting your high school diploma or a GED is imperative these days. Almost every job requires one. If your guidance counselor isn't able to help you, then a therapist or social worker might have ideas and strategies that will guide you back on course. Do your best to try, try again. Reevaluate and reset your goals and priorities—school, job, and so on.

(If something like substance abuse is a factor in your being thrown out of school, or failing out, then look to future chapters for more information on treatment.)

Problems at Work

Not getting along with coworkers or your boss is definitely something that can cause you to feel down. Since we spend the majority of our waking hours at work as adults, and the majority of your "free time" as a teen might be spent working part time, when you are unhappy in your work environment, it could be cause for concern. You may want to reevaluate the job you have chosen. Perhaps it's not the right job for you or even the right company. Deciding to quit a job, though stressful, should be taken seriously. It could make all the difference in your moods. Think of another place you could work that would make you happy and fulfilled, a place where you are excited to go each day.

Being fired, downsized, terminated, whatever the technical term used, can all mean the same thing: feelings of low self-worth. Sometime you know you are not suited for a job, and being fired isn't a huge surprise, but it still hurts. Other times, you can be "let go" without seeing it coming, and this can cause a feeling of hopelessness and devastation. It's hard not to take it personally! But you need to dust yourself off and try again. There's more than one job, and even career path, for everyone. All you can do is try your best. A helpful idea is to find a mentor, ask lots of questions, and see if a certain career path is right for you. Each experience, whether good or bad, will give you some kind of personal education. There are lessons to be learned in everyday life.

Problems with Money

Whether your family has had low income or has lost an income because of the recession, poverty can be a potent trigger for depression. Worrying about money for bills, food, and clothing can be a huge stress, especially for young people who feel they have very little control to help the situation. Even if you are old enough to hold a job, having to help support a family at such a young age can cause a myriad of feelings from concern and worry to resentment. It can all be so confusing, battling a variety of emotions, most of which can involve fear—fear for the present day, along with fear for your future. Anxiety and worry are emotions often tangled up with depression. Anxiety is a related illness (mood disorder) to depression, and each can aggravate the other.

Illness of You or Someone You Love

If you've been diagnosed with a serious or chronic illness, or if your mortality is in question, you may be dealing with depression. It can be overwhelming to be young and have to deal with something such as diabetes, cancer, or cystic fibrosis, just to name a few. You will undoubtedly receive pamphlets from your physician on how to cope with your illness, and information about possible support groups.

Basic Techniques to Help with Depression Triggers

- Practicing positive "self-talk" (i.e., I *can* do it. I *will* get the job/part in the play/a passing grade . . . fill in the blank).
- Seeking the help of a counselor, social worker, or psychiatrist.
- Maintaining a healthy lifestyle—Exercise regularly, and no smoking, no drinking alcohol, and no excessive junk food eating.
- Resting—Get a full night's sleep whenever possible, without falling into the habit of oversleeping, or napping too much. (Oversleeping can be a symptom of depression.)
- Hydrating—Drink plenty of water, and avoid caffeine and other stimulants.

For more ideas, see chapter 11, "Healthy Coping Mechanisms."

If the one who is sick is not you, but someone you love, this can be very traumatic as well. If a sibling or a parent has been diagnosed with heart problems, diabetes, or even cancer, this can bring up questions you never thought of before, such as "What would I do without that person?" These are serious issues that could require psychological help or possibly a medical intervention. Be sure to take advantage of any help that is offered to you.

When is there a connection between illness and depression? If you have chronic pain, that could lead to depression. However, sometimes the treatments for illness, such as certain medications, can cause a depression. If you are taking opiod medicines like oxycodone or morphine to manage your pain, the side effect could be depression.[7] Other drugs that might cause depression are muscle relaxants or illegal drugs, such as amphetamines like crystal meth.

Grief—Death of Someone You Know

Illness, accidents, old age, and suicide are all causes of death that can catch you by surprise. Often when death is expected or unexpected, it can create a tailspin in your life and throw you into a depression. Death is never easy to experience at any age, but it's especially tough in adolescence. This is partly because it may be your first experience with death firsthand. You may have never been to a wake or a funeral, and it can be scary and overwhelming. As a kid, you have a feeling of being invincible and cannot fully comprehend the danger in certain situations. (Risky behaviors will be discussed in chapter 5, "Unhealthy Coping Mechanisms.") Being able to comprehend the finality of death can seem nearly impossible.

Sometimes dealing with the loss of someone you know or love can be too much to bear, especially if you've lost more than one person to death within a short period of time. When you think of your own life's problems, if you've ever considered something as extreme as suicide, please reconsider the finality of it all. Problems come and go, but death is forever. A life is a precious thing, and even if

❗ Understanding Your Feelings of Grief

According to Helen Fitzgerald, author of *The Grieving Teen: A Guide for Teenagers and Their Friends*, the depression that is experienced during the grieving process could be referred to as "bereavement depression" and can show up in anyone who cared for the person who has died. The length and severity varies from person to person, but generally lasts only a few hours to a few days. If it goes on for more than two weeks, then a serious clinical depression could be diagnosed.[e]

you don't feel especially fortunate to be alive, there will come a time again when you will experience joy, friendship, success, and love.

Life is made up of ups and downs, and things will not always be so traumatic and horrible as they may seem to you at any given time. You have to practice positive self-talk, and try to psych yourself up. Saying things as simple as "I *will* get a new job," or "I *will* go back to school," or even "I *will* repair my relationship with my parent" and repeating them daily, if necessary, can help set your mood and attitude. Having feelings of gratitude for what is going well can help you feel hopeful and even optimistic.

Remembering how quickly life and its events can change should give you a feeling of "What if?" And isn't that one of the best parts of life: "What if I make the team?" "What if he asks me out?" "What if I get a part in the play?" "What if I get a scholarship?" Sure, you can fill your head with the opposite/negative talk, but why? Don't feed into that inner voice that is full of negative talk. It does no good. I realize it's easier said than done sometimes, but make a conscious effort to have the positive reinforcement talks with yourself. It takes effort, but it's worth it!

Comparing Self to Others: Siblings and Birth Order

Common personality traits have been linked to birth order. An interesting article titled "Does Birth Order Really Matter?" by Sue Flanagan and Patty Morrison, on the West Virginia University Extension Services' website, discusses this topic. In the article, it says that it is a commonly known fact that a large number of presidents of the United States have been firstborns or only children in their families.

Firstborn (and only children) receive the most undistracted attention from the parents, at least until another child arrives. Therefore, they are often very successful, have great leadership qualities, can be conservative, organized, and responsible.

Middle children often have to seek acceptance or validation from peers, because they are in the shadow of an older sibling, or in competition with an attention-seeking youngest child. Middle children have been noted to be very social, competitive, generous, peacemakers, and they maintain strong friendships.

The youngest child in a family usually gets the most attention from both the parents and the other siblings in the family. This can sometimes cause them to be spoiled or manipulative. However, they can also be characterized as charming, affectionate, persistent, uncertain, and attention loving.[8]

No matter where you fall in your family dynamic, you have struggles of your own and may become depressed. It is a possible side effect of any of the birth order scenarios. It's not easy to be in any family, and when you have siblings to contend with for attention, affection, and recognition, that can weigh heavily on a

Setting Priorities and Goals for Yourself

Identify what is positive in your life right now, in the moment. Identifying life goals is the heart of the (depression) recovery process. When we see a future for ourselves, we begin to become motivated to do all we can to reach that future. Goals can be big or small, depending on where you are in your recovery journey. (Check out *Reaching Your Goals: The Ultimate Teen Guide* [2009], a book in this It Happened to Me series from Scarecrow Press, to learn more about goal setting.)

Ask yourself,

- What motivates me?
- What interests me?
- What would I do more of if I could?
- What do I want?
- What do I care about, or what did I care about before my illness?
- Where do I want my life to go?
- What brings me joy?
- What are my dreams and hopes?
- What can I change in my life? (How can I feel empowered?)

It can help to start small and work up to larger goals. You might want to begin by setting one small goal for yourself at the beginning of each day. As you move forward with your recovery, look at the different areas of your life and think about your short- and long-term goals. (We will look at setting specific goals in chapter 12, "Healthy Coping Mechanisms.")

Whether you achieve one small goal per day or are checking off a long list of larger goals, the fact that you are making an effort is something to be proud of!

young person. Perhaps you are an only child, and that makes you lonely at times. By noticing personality traits that are common per birth order, you can make conscious efforts to strengthen your positive qualities and diminish your weaknesses.

Comparing Self to Others: Peers

While you love your friends—truly you do—it's hard not to compare yourself to them sometimes, right? You might have a friend that always gets straight As at school, while you struggle to occasionally make the honor roll. And then there's that friend who always looks so amazing with her stylish clothes and perfect hair and makeup. You look like something the cat dragged in a lot of the time. Why do we, as humans, constantly compare ourselves to others? Who knows! But I do know that trying to measure up to someone else's standards all of the time is not something that is going to help your self-esteem. By constantly comparing yourself, and feeling you don't always measure up, you can become depressed.

Have you ever heard the phrase "keeping up with the Joneses"? It means you are so preoccupied with doing what everyone else in the neighborhood is doing that you've stopped thinking about yourself, your standards, and your beliefs. You just want to copy those who are popular. Don't think that you're alone in this action; adults do it too. But it is a habit that you can break with practice. Think to yourself, "Who do *I* want to be? What do *I* believe is the right way to be, act, or look?" Then make decisions for yourself based on your *own* feelings, not your friends' actions and beliefs.

As a teen, you've probably figured out that you're well on your way to adulthood. It can be exciting and scary at the same time. Being grown up gives you freedoms you don't particularly have right now, but it also comes with responsibilities. Take things slowly, and you will adjust to all the changes in due time.

Belittling or Criticism by Adult Role Model (Parent, Teacher, Coach, Relative)

Belittling or criticizing someone is a form of emotional abuse. Emotional abuse by a parent or other authority figure can cripple a young person's self-esteem. Teenagers are often at odds with adults over a difference of opinion over grades, clothing, makeup, and especially friends they choose to hang around with. However, it is usually a matter of growing pains and finding your own voice. When a person of authority is truly abusive, by belittling or constantly criticizing you, it may lead to an internal struggle that you may not know how to deal with. Have you found such a situation to bring on a depressive episode? Ideally, an adult—especially a parent—should be a cheerleader for you, or at least seem to be on

Bounce-Back Strategies

Try one of these when you feel you're sliding into a depression:

- Take a walk or do some other form of exercise.
- Watch a funny movie.
- Eat comfort food (without overdoing it, of course!).
- Hang out with friends.
- Make up a code word—for example, when you're having a rough day but don't necessarily want to talk at the moment, you can text a friend something like "Chill" or random words like "Peanut butter," and he'll know you're reaching out, but to check back with you later.
- Reach out to people in the moment—call or text a friend or IM someone if you just need to feel that connection to another person.
- Download Headspace, which is a meditation app for iPhone.
- Watch YouTube videos on meditation.

your side. When you don't get the proper support from your adult role model, your feelings of doubt or worthlessness can creep in. Finding a supportive adult you can trust and confide in, whether it is a coach, a teacher, a religious leader, a friend's parent, a neighbor, or even an aunt or uncle, can help with your emotional well-being. Finding someone to believe in you is essential to your peace of mind.

Violence in American Culture: News, TV, and Movies

The Internet and American media culture (TV, movies, music) are full of disturbing images that may trigger a depression and/or anxiety in everyone, especially young people. Images of violence and even death can be confusing and disheartening. You cannot always know how to process all of the images thrown at you at your age (at any age, in some cases.)

According to an online article in *Pediatrics* (the official journal of the American Academy of Pediatrics), exposure to violence in the media represents a significant risk to the health of children and adolescents. Extensive research shows that media violence can contribute to aggressive behavior, desensitization to violence,

> ### ! Real Statistic–Real Concerns
>
> By eighteen years of age, the average young person will have viewed approximately 200,000 acts of violence on television alone. That doesn't account for video games, movies, and Internet sites![f]
>
> Research has associated exposure to media violence with a variety of physical and mental health problems for children and adolescents. Some problems include aggressive and violent behavior, bullying, desensitization to violence, fear, depression, nightmares, and sleep disturbances. Some children have even shown anxiety, PTSD, and/or social isolation from exposure to media violence.[9]

nightmares, and fear of being harmed.[9] The medical community has been concerned with this issue since the 1950s.[10]

What Can Shield Me from the Violence?

What's important for you to know is that you can shield yourself from a lot of media violence by just saying no. *Don't* turn on the news, *don't* buy the newest CD with "Parental Warnings," *don't* go see the newest NC-17 rated movie. Take yourself out of the equation of exposure to violence. Murder is casually displayed all over the television for anyone to see, and many cable shows, which are not rated or monitored, do not prevent a young person's viewing (unless your parents use parental-control options available on some television systems). While it may seem silly to you, since "it's just pretend" in a lot of cases, like some crazy slasher movies, many of the horrors shown can seem all too real when you're lying in bed, trying to fall asleep!

By focusing on more positive images, scenes, and ideas, you will give yourself more positive thoughts. Perhaps you've never thought of it, but consider reading a self-help book or an inspirational website on the Internet. Do something positive for yourself each day. You can try something more soothing, like meditation, before bed instead of falling asleep with the television on in the background. This can certainly help create a lighter mood, rather than focusing on all the negative things that can happen in the world.

Cyber-Abuse/Social Media

With technology so advanced today, teens can cyber-abuse each other by using things such as social media and other Internet avenues, cruel and/or bullying

National Comorbidity Survey–Adolescent Supplement

Approximately 11 percent of adolescents have a depressive disorder by age eighteen.[h]

texts, tweets, and de-friending on Facebook. If you are being bullied, this can be a traumatic source of what triggers your depression.

According to the Academy of Pediatrics, social media can be a positive thing in helping adolescents with communication, social interactions, and a sense of community. However, it can also become a negative with sites like Facebook (having a number of friends publicly, or *not* having many friends) and can lead to low self-esteem and peer pressure, which can worsen anxiety or depression.[11]

The American Academy of Pediatrics also notes that online cyberbullying and harassment "can cause profound psychosocial outcomes including depression, anxiety, severe isolation, and, tragically, suicide."[12]

Has someone ever sent out pix of you online or said mean things about you on the web? This can not only devastate a person emotionally, but permanently harm one's reputation as well. Things can stay on the World Wide Web forever. When looking for a job or applying to college, you don't want any random photos of you in compromising positions to show up in a search done by prospective employers or universities.

Compromising photos can harm someone the other way as well. Have *you* ever "tagged" a person in a photo without asking for his permission? Sure it may have been at a fun party you attended with your friend, but such pictures, while

Could High Internet Use Cause Depression in Youth?

There was a Chinese study published August 2, 2010, in the *Archives of Pediatrics and Adolescent Medicine*, which followed 1,041 high school students' activities on the Internet. What they found was that teens who were free of anxiety and depression at the start of the study, and were "pathological Internet users," had achieved rates of severe depression 2.5 times higher than those of other students after only nine months. At the end of the nine-month study, 8.4 percent of the subjects developed mild to severe depression.

Dr. Lawrence T. Lam, of the School of Medicine in Sydney, Australia, speculated that high Internet users often went days or weeks without getting enough sleep, which can contribute to depression.[i]

seemingly harmless, could resurface at a much later time and be inappropriate and harmful to another person's reputation. Always ask permission before putting anything out in cyberspace.

Emotional Abuse in Relationships

Relationships with the opposite sex, or same sex if gay, can be highly emotional in adolescence. Your hormones are still adjusting to going through, or having gone through, puberty. Therefore, dealing with a love interest can be tricky at times, especially if you're prone to depressive episodes.

When teens find that "first love" they sometimes feel they will do *anything* for the other person, to show how much they care. This may or may not always be in one's own best interest. Sometimes people feel pressured to have sex before they are ready, or at least to do more physically than they feel emotionally ready to handle on their own.

A boyfriend might pressure his girlfriend into doing something physical by saying, "If you *really* love me, you will . . . [fill in the blank]" or might go so far as to say, "There are plenty of other girls at this school who would love to be in your position. I can easily hook up with them, if you're not willing to prove your love." This is emotional abuse and may even trigger your depression.

Emotional abuse can go both ways, guys to girls, or girls to guys. For example, a girl might say, "Why don't you want to sleep with me? Aren't you a man? I'm going to tell everyone what a total wimp you are." Sure this is extreme, but it could happen.

Other ways boyfriends and girlfriends can abuse each other emotionally is to talk down to one another, chipping away at each other's self-worth, therefore triggering a depression. Always putting someone down is a horrible thing to do to someone you "love," yet it happens all the time. For example, a guy might say, "Wow, you look so skanky. Why did you buy *those* new clothes?" or "Why do you eat so much crap? You look like a fat pig." And young women can be equally volatile by saying something like "Why don't you ever work out? You're so thin and weak!" or "C'mon, just chug this beer. *Real* men can hold their liquor!"

These are examples of emotional abuse that when they go on repeatedly, can fracture a person's soul. If you're constantly belittled, it's hard not to start believing what you're told. Such comments can become negative "inner voices" in your head, repeating such put-downs that you've heard over and over again! Negative inner thoughts are a symptom of depression.

If you find yourself being emotionally abused, do your best to gather your strength and leave the situation. A person who truly loves you will not ever make you feel like less of a person, period!

Physical Abuse and Depression

Physical abuse can be a part of your life through your family, a "friend," or a romantic interest, and it is *never* okay. Feeling things like "he didn't mean to" or "it was just one time" are not acceptable feelings. Your health and mental well-being are at stake! You don't want such a situation to trigger a depression. There are support groups to help you get out of situations that endanger your life and mental health. Such groups that meet and have local chapters include the following:

- Adult Survivors of Child Abuse (ASCA) (www.ascasupport.org)
- Co-Dependents Anonymous (CODA) (www.coda.org)
- Daily Strength (http://www.dailystrength.org/c/Physical-Emotional -Abuse/support-group)
- General abuse support groups in your area (www.abusesupportgroups.com)
- PsychCentral (www.psychcentral.com/resources/Abuse/Support_Groups)

Sexual Abuse and Depression

Sexual abuse can repeat itself in a never-ending cycle if not acknowledged and treated. You do not want to fall into this horrific trap. If you are being abused

"Escape." *Photo courtesy of Heather Schwartz*

by someone you know, you need to report it. Fear is often a factor in not telling of the abuse, but it can cause irreversible damage to your physical and emotional well-being. Even if you don't report it to authorities, you should seek a doctor's exam, along with personal counseling for your own health reasons. Such abuse can easily trigger a depression. There are anonymous hotlines available with counselors you can speak to, as well as websites with live chats, and helpful information. Here are some of them:

- National Domestic Violence/Abuse Hotline, www.allaboutcounseling .com/sexual_abuse.htm, 1-800-799-SAFE
- RAINN (Rape, Abuse, and Incest National Network), www.rainn.org, 800-856-HOPE
- Safe Help Line (confidential live chat for sexual assault survivors in the military), www.safehelpline.org, 877-995-5247
- National Domestic Violence Hotline, www.thehotline.org (1-800-787-3224)
- National Child Abuse Hotline, www.ChildHelp.org/pages/hotline-home (accessed May 30, 2014) 1-800-4-A-CHILD (1-800-422-4453)
  - Dating Violence (1-866-331-9474) has twenty-four-hour peer advocates
  - National Center for Victims of Crimes Stalking Resource Center is available Monday through Friday, 8:30 a.m. to 8:30 p.m., EST (1-800-FYI-CALL.)

3

INTERNAL (OR BIOCHEMICAL) TRIGGERS OF YOUR DEPRESSION

What Does *Internal Triggers* Mean?

When I talk about *internal triggers* in this chapter, and perhaps other spots within this book, I mean things that cause you to have depressive feelings that are out of your control—internally. Examples include biological factors, such as your hereditary makeup, or physiological issues, such as neurotransmitter issues, menstrual factors for women, learning disabilities, and physical disabilities.

Although the causes of depression are not understood fully, we will explore the internal triggers that might be responsible for your depressive moods or your vulnerability to them. Family history is often considered. Depression may seem to be inherited in some children. Here are some internal reasons a person could become depressed.

Heredity—Child or Relative of a Depressed Person

Could your depression be something that has been passed on to you from a parent or other relative? Depressive illnesses are disorders of the brain.[1] Changes in the body's balance of hormones may be possible triggers of depression as well. It makes sense that if major depressive disorders are possibly biological, genetic factors could be passed down from parent to child. If a family member does have a major depressive disorder, it is not, however, a certainty that you will have it, too.

In the book *Contemporary Issues Companion: Depression*, it states that people who have family members with major depression are up to three times more likely to develop a disorder.[2] According to the American Psychiatric Association's

Triggers out of your control.

DSM-5 (*Diagnostic and Statistical Manual of Mental Disorders*), immediate family members of those with a major depressive disorder have a risk factor two- to fourfold higher than someone in the general population. Also, it was noted that there are relative risks higher for early-onset depression and recurrent forms of the disorder.[3]

Oftentimes, you may never have talked about or even acknowledged your parent or other family member's depression. It is common for it to be an unspoken "family secret." Do you know if your relative is depressed, or is it something you suspect? You may want to ask your parent about it or even the person you suspect is depressed. You could voice your concern for her health, along with your own concerns about your symptoms of depression. Let your relative know that your depression could be hereditary, and any information she feels comfortable sharing would be appreciated.

The subject of depression should come up at your yearly physical with your doctor as well. You could tell him about any symptoms you are having, and tell him anything you might know about your family history. While the physician would not know about a relative's medical history, he may be able to give an opinion on whether he feels depression might be a hereditary concern for you, from the information you've provided.

The easiest and best place to start learning about your family's medical history is by simply being open with your relative if you suspect she may have depression in her DNA. There are other resources for family members and friends of someone who is depressed. If you google "depression support" or some form of question regarding depression, you will get a variety of national and local groups, many of which are listed in the back matter of this book. Starting to look at yourself, and not your family history, might be an option you are more comfortable with at the moment. That is fine, too. Two resources that have a wealth of information about depression are NAMI (National Alliance of Mental Illness) and DBSA (Depression Bipolar Support Alliance).

"Self-Portrait—Eyes: A Look into the Soul, 'Am I Depressed?'" *Photo courtesy of Heather Schwartz.*

Premenstrual Syndrome

There are some symptoms females deal with all month that get exacerbated approximately five days before menstruation starts, and last until a few days after the menstruation has begun. Some women do not have these symptoms at all during other times of the month. These women who *only* have symptoms in the days leading up to their period are categorized as having what is commonly known as premenstrual syndrome, or PMS. There is controversy surrounding how the syndrome should be categorized. According to Francis Mark Mondimore, MD, in his book *Depression: The Mood Disease*, the American Psychiatric Association debated adding PMS as a diagnostic category. Studies that have attempted to define the syndrome range greatly in description depending on who conducts the study. For example, gynecologists focus on the physical symptoms. Psychologists and psychiatrists study the emotional symptoms, whereas endocrinologists try to note the hormone levels. There have been a total of 150 symptoms considered to vary with the menstrual cycle.[4] Some of the symptoms noted are bloating, irritability, depression or mood swings, and cramping, just to name a few.

Postpartum Depression for Teen Moms

With many teen pregnancies, it is important to know about another depression which follows childbirth called postpartum depression (PPD). For young women, it can manifest itself in behaviors such as uncontrollable crying up to something as severe as psychosis. If people tell you, "It's just the 'baby blues' and not to worry about it," don't take that to heart, especially if you find yourself crying a lot, and feeling isolated and uncontrollably sad. If you feel you are more down than usual, or have irrational thoughts of harming yourself or your child, please seek immediate help from 9-1-1. You can also seek help from your doctor, a counselor, a religious figure, a trusted friend, a family member, or a neighbor.

In 2001 Marie Osmond, along with Marcia Wilkie and Dr. Judith Moore, wrote a self-help book titled *Behind the Smile: My Journey out of Postpartum Depression*. Osmond had very publicly dealt with severe PPD. In the book, she shares her experiences with having seven children, having a marriage that endured a public separation, and having a high-profile career in show business—all at the same time. She was lucky to have a support group of loved ones who helped her deal with the stressors. Her coauthors also wrote chapters about PPD risk factors to watch for along with recommended reading.

Later, in 2005, following the release of actress Brooke Shields's book *Down Came the Rain: My Journey through Postpartum Depression*, Shields had a very public spat with actor Tom Cruise, over a treatment she was receiving for her PPD.

Cruise stated that medications such as antidepressants were unnecessary and that Shields could be cured by taking vitamins instead. He went on the *Today* show with Matt Lauer and triggered a huge debate over this. Much press was given to this interview, questioning Cruise and his strong beliefs that are part of his association with Scientology.

Many people seem to have very strong beliefs when it comes to postpartum and other forms of depression. For some reason, they feel the need to share such opinions as if they were experts (as Cruise seemed to do with Matt Lauer). However, it is important for you to turn a deaf ear to such people and rely heavily on the trained professionals who can help you, such as a therapist, psychiatrist, or your family physician. They are trained to help with such conditions and are not just acting on opinions. They will have your best interest at heart and may possibly be able to help you the most.

Learning Disabilities

While many learning disabled teens are "mainstreamed" into the general population classrooms, they still feel stigmatized by having an aide, or being labeled as learning disabled. Problems such as ADD (attention deficit disorder) or ADHD (attention-deficit/hyperactivity disorder), or such disorders as dyslexia or autism can make teens stand out when they don't necessarily want to. There is the pressure for teens to perform at the level that their classmates or coworkers do, people who do not have such disabilities to contend with. The disabled teens might not feel socially accepted. When teens have problems acting out in class or at work, this only worsens the stigma of being different. Some of these teens have to deal with social rejection at school, neglect, or teasing.[5] Having learning disorders can also be a source of teen depression, although the studies have not been done as extensively on this group of teens.

Physical Disabilities

Teens who have physical disabilities either from birth or later onset may have to deal with additional obstacles. The life they are faced with often comes with burdens such as anxiety and/or depression.[6]

In a 2002 study published in the *Oxford Journal of Pediatric Psychology*, doctors explored the self-perceived quality of life of middle and high schoolers with and without disabilities. The results showed that teens with disabilities reported lower quality of life, including depressive symptoms, than teens without disabilities. The findings suggest that reducing social and environmental barriers and including

Steven's Story: Living with Cerebral Palsy

As a teenager, depression became part of Steven's life, dealing with his own physical disability of having cerebral palsy and watching his dad suffer from severe manic depression [bipolar].

"I was an outcast at school. My sister and I didn't get along. My Special Education teachers in high school kept me isolated. I was mainstreamed taking regular classes, but when my teachers assigned class work, I had to leave the classroom to return to the special ed classroom to dictate my assignments [so I wouldn't disrupt my "regular" classmates]."

Having the worries at home about his father's ailment and suicide attempts was a trigger for Steven's own depression. He explains how it spiraled down.

"After graduating from high school with honors, I sat at home for two years doing nothing. Being labeled unable to work by the government [due to my cerebral palsy] really destroyed me. All I wanted to do was to go to college, but the government didn't believe that I could do anything and paying for college and technology output devices was out of the question. During that Christmastime, my dad died. I was completely lost falling into a deep depression, but I kept moving forward like I do now."[a]

young people with disabilities in school, family, and community activities could possibly improve the quality of life of these teens.[7]

Being accepted by other people is a natural desire for all humans, and teens seem to seek this out more than most age groups—acceptance by peers. If we stop segregating teens with disabilities (either by accident, or intentionally) it could help their overall quality of life, whether real or perceived.

Neurotransmitter Issues

Another internal trigger that links to depression could be dealing with neurotransmitter issues. Neurotransmitters are naturally occurring brain chemicals that assist in transmitting messages between nerve cells in the brain.[8] Some of these chemicals are responsible for a person's moods. If there is an imbalance of chemicals (such as dopamine, norepinephrine, and/or serotonin), depression can occur.[9] Simply by having a chemical imbalance, a person can feel depressed due

"You fall into a depression slowly, like a building burns. It starts as a spark so small, it would not even be dangerous in itself. But fire needs fuel. The spark would not spread without a piece of paper next to it to cling on to. The fire spreads to the table. It moves onto the floor. And sooner or later you're standing there, and your lungs are screaming and your skin feels like it's melting, and the only thing that's on your mind, is that you need to get out."—Anonymous teen, excerpt from "I Beat Depression" featured in *TeenInk.com*[b]

to this internal trigger. It may have nothing to do with any external trigger such as a romantic relationship ending, death of a loved one, doing poorly at school, or some other intense situation. People may spontaneously be depressed due to their chemical makeup.

It is important to know that teenagers sometimes react to the pain of depression by getting into trouble—using alcohol, drugs, or sex to cope with negative feelings.[10] They may also get into trouble at school, or start getting bad grades, or have problems with family or friends. These troubles are examples of reasons to seek help and get treated if you feel you might be depressed. Before your troubles start to feel really out of control, get help from a professional![11]

The theory behind physicians prescribing antidepressants is that these medications could ease the depression experienced by people if the drugs can adjust the supply of certain neurotransmitters in the brain. For example, one type of antidepressant increases your brain's level of norepinephrine, while another type stops the breakdown of norepinephrine.[12] It is a complicated balance of chemicals in the brain, and therefore getting just the right medication and dosage can be a challenge.

While neurotransmitters can often be the culprit of depression, it is also believed that the receptors, which are what receive the information, may also be responsible.[13] If a receptor is damaged or broken, then naturally the message will be incorrect. This error in the receipt of information is what can ultimately cause a depression.

OTHER MOOD DISORDERS (DEPRESSION-RELATED ILLNESSES)

Anxiety Disorders

There is a long list of anxiety disorders, including panic attacks, social phobia, obsessive-compulsive disorder, acute stress disorder, generalized anxiety disorder, and substance-induced anxiety disorder, to name a few. To avoid a lengthy list of multiple conditions, this book will focus on generalized anxiety disorder.

Often with depression, there can be an overlapping of anxiety as a symptom, or an actual anxiety disorder. Unlike the common anxiety experienced by most people briefly when experiencing stressful events such as public speaking, or a first date, anxiety disorders last at least six months and can get worse if they are not treated.[1] There is a booklet by the National Institute of Mental Health that shares information on symptoms and solutions to the following problems: anxiety disorders, generalized anxiety disorder, obsessive-compulsive disorder, panic disorder, post-traumatic stress disorder, and social phobia.[2] Generalized anxiety may be due to the feelings of worthlessness, helplessness, and hopelessness that can occur with depression. In a study by psychiatrist Maurizio Fava, MD, of Harvard, he reported that 51 percent of those in the study were found to have anxiety along with their depression. It is not certain if they are directly related, as 40 percent of those in the anxiety/depression study stated their anxiety disorder started first.[3]

Anxiety disorders may show up early in life, during childhood, due to abnormally high levels of hormones driving the body's stress response system.[4] Anxiety compounded with symptoms of depression can make treatment difficult.

In addition to counseling or psychotherapy, some physicians may prescribe a combination of medications, perhaps an antianxiety medication such as Xanax

When you just don't feel "right" . . .

> ### Anxiety Disorders
>
> According to the *DSM-5* (*Diagnostic and Statistical Manual of Mental Disorders*), "Anxiety disorders include disorders that share features of excessive fear and anxiety and related behavioral disturbances. *Fear* is the emotional response to real or perceived imminent threat, whereas *anxiety* is anticipation of future threat."[a]

(alprazolam) or Ativan (lorazepam) *and* an antidepressant. If you feel you may be suffering from an anxiety disorder and/or depression, visiting a psychiatrist for a diagnosis might be helpful to you. Psychiatrists are usually the ones who prescribe medications and psychotherapy for these conditions, if they deem it necessary.

Bipolar Disorder

One definition of bipolar disorder found on *Merriam-Webster's* online medical dictionary is "any of several mood disorders characterized usually by alternating episodes of depression and mania, or by episodes of depression alternating with mild nonpsychotic excitement."[5]

In his book *Depression: The Mood Disease*, Francis Mark Mondimore, MD, defines bipolar disorder as a mixed affective state, saying that the mood has qualities of both major depression and the manic state.[6]

While there can be many causes for bipolar disorder, it is most likely from genetic reasons.[7] Of those people with bipolar disorder, it is ten times more common for a blood relative to also have the disorder than someone in the general population.[8] People who have the disorder show symptoms at a much earlier age than in the past. This could be due to stresses not as common in previous generations, such as divorce, single-parent homes, and having to move more frequently. Drug and alcohol dependency play a large role as well.[9]

Some symptoms of bipolar disorder's manic phases are

- an unusually "high" or euphoric feeling, where everything seems super-great and you are almost too giddy to contain yourself.
- feeling edgy or irritable instead of euphoric, where every little thing annoys you. You may even be hypersensitive to things like sound and the noises around you.
- unusually high self-esteem. This is where you are over the top with self-confidence, where you feel your abilities to change things, or even ideas you have, are completely brilliant and extraordinary. You seem to think others are just unable to see your superiority, and you might even feel you have a great deal in common with famous people.
- racing thoughts. You have a hard time focusing on one particular point, your thoughts are all over the place, and people may have a hard time following a conversation with you.
- being more vocal and outspoken. You may be talking more quickly or loudly than usual, where others in a conversation can't get a word in edgewise. You may be talking too much and even talking about inappropriate things.
- needing less sleep than usual. You have more energy and feel more alert than normal, wanting to make plans and do things that are so exciting that you don't want to waste a single moment with something as trivial as sleeping.
- being easily distracted. You cannot seem to focus, and background noises such as the television or a phone ringing in the distance can take away your train of thought.
- an increased sex drive. You may seem to want sex all the time with your partner, or even have risky behaviors such as multiple partners in a short period of time.

- being hyperactive with extra ability for starting lots of different activities or assignments. Some might feel you are overextending yourself. You may be working on a number of projects at work and home, but unable to finish any of them.
- self-destructive or impulsive behavior. You may be taking more risks than normal such as multiple sexual partners, overspending money, abusing substances such as drugs and/or alcohol. Your impulse control (or not thinking of consequences) is out of whack. While others may be cautioning your behaviors, you feel they are just worrying for nothing or being too uptight.[10]

> "From a very young age I noticed certain things . . . then in the 8th grade, I saw an on-line class Dad took, and the book on bipolar. Things suddenly started to make sense."—William, age 19[b]

If you see yourself in any of these behaviors, it is important that you contact a physician, psychiatrist, or therapist. You may be experiencing mania.

Depression symptoms are listed in chapter 1. If you feel you may have mania combined with depression, seeing a doctor for diagnosis is key for finding treatment. Bipolar disorder may be the cause of such symptoms.

Dysthymia Disorder

Dysthymia is a less severe depression than major depression. However, it is a long-term condition that can hinder a person from feeling well or being as productive as possible. It does not completely disable a person, as a major depression can, but it is chronic.[11] In fact, those who suffer from dysthymia *and* a major depression simultaneously are diagnosed with *double depression*. This occurs in up to 70 percent of dysthymic patients.[12]

> "After I survived my Dad's first suicide attempt, my family—mom and my sister—lived with his depression for two years. We endured eight more suicide attempts in those years until he moved to Oakland to live with his sister. We couldn't take his depression anymore. It was like living on pins and needles not knowing what my dad might do at anytime."
> —Steven, adult looking back on his teen years[c]

> ### ! What Other Diseases Can Trigger Depression?
>
> Attention-deficit/hyperactivity disorder, diabetes, cancer, multiple sclerosis, cystic fibrosis, and fibromyalgia are all examples of diseases that might cause depression, either as part of the symptoms or merely from having such a serious disease. It can be overwhelming to deal with the day-to-day stresses of having any of these diagnoses.

Dysthymia is often diagnosed in patients who also have AIDS, chronic fatigue syndrome, diabetes, hypothyroidism, and multiple sclerosis.[13] It is not clear exactly why two conditions are often in tandem. However, the link may be due to how the drugs used to treat the conditions affect the brain's neurotransmitters,[14] which are chemicals in the brain responsible for carrying out commands from the brain to the body.

Other disorders commonly found in dysthymic disorder patients are panic disorders, personality disorders, social phobias, substance abuse, and other psychiatric conditions.[15]

Premenstrual Dysphoric Disorder

Another depressive illness related to hormones is known as PMDD, or premenstrual dysphoric disorder. Some of the symptoms can include anger, anxiety, fatigue, irritableness, sadness, crying, withdrawal, feelings of guilt, and/or feelings of self-loathing.[16]

There are differences between PMDD and premenstrual syndrome (PMS). PMDD is a severe, sometimes disabling extension of PMS.[17] PMDD is associated with the hormonal changes that typically occur around ovulation and before menstruation begins, therefore, occurring at a concurrent time to PMS, but much more serious.[18]

As a teen, you might ask your health class teacher for information or guidance with possible depression issues, especially if you don't want to go to your doctor right away. Health class can be a beginning step to investigate your questions more closely.

Psychotic Depression

According to the National Institute of Mental Health, "Psychotic depression occurs when a person has severe depression, plus some form of psychosis, such as having disturbing false beliefs or a break with reality (delusions), or hears or sees upsetting things that others cannot hear or see (hallucinations)."[19]

Seasonal Affective Disorder

SAD, or seasonal affective disorder, is a condition that usually begins in fall or winter and tapers off in the spring. This usually occurs at times of the year when there are low levels of sunlight. Young people are more prone to SAD, and women tend to be more susceptible to it than men.[20] The symptoms of SAD may be the same as a major depressive episode, or they may be more mild. When there is more sunlight, as in the spring, this disorder lifts.

What can you do to help relieve the symptoms of this disorder? Light therapy tends to be a successful treatment, and can show signs of working in approximately two weeks. It is a strict regimen of sitting close to a specific lamp with a certain wavelength, for almost two hours per day. Some teens and adults find this too time-consuming to stick to.[21]

Others choose to try medications to control their seasonal affective disorder. Antidepressants are an option that has been shown to be successful.[22] Lastly, to get through SAD during the fall and winter months, some seek psychotherapy. Having a therapist talk through your feelings and ask thought-provoking questions can be beneficial. This and other therapies will be discussed in further chapters as well.

UNHEALTHY COPING MECHANISMS

The teen years can include a combination of becoming more independent from your family, while also trying to fit in with your peers. With the pressure to fit in and the stresses of everyday life such as school, work, socialization, home life, friendships, social networking, and other responsibilities, teens and young adults have a lot of everyday worries. Without a strong support system, many can fall into bad habits, or "unhealthy coping mechanisms," to try and deal with their problems.

When the stress of depression seems to be just too much to bear, young adults or teens can fall into some bad habits such as "self-medicating" themselves with

Self-medicating to numb the pain.

alcohol, marijuana, or even prescription drugs. Some can succumb to eating disorders such as anorexia and/or bulimia. Cutting, other self-mutilation, and more self-destructive behaviors are some of the problems that can be brought on by depression. Another equally unhealthy coping mechanism is doing harm to others. This might include picking fights, bullying, and wanting to seriously hurt others, as seen in tragic events like school shootings. Another extreme behavior is suicide attempts.

Untitled

Happy clouds form magical pictures
Children chasing the end of the rainbow
I want to be there
I want the pot of gold
All I found was gravel
I crawl in the dirt
It's soft and cool and dark
The darkness comforts me
My bare skin turning dirty
I wait for someone to lend a hand
To pull me out
Pull me out

—Christina, age 17[1]

Alcohol and Other Substance Abuse

When young people are upset or depressed, many choose to numb their pain with alcohol. This helps temporarily, until the alcohol has its full effect as a depressant. Then the drinkers need more alcohol to feel the numbing sensation, before their moods drop again, this time lower. It's a terrible cycle that goes deeper and deeper, worsening the depression.

American teens' top drug of choice is alcohol.[2] According to the Center on Addiction and Substance Abuse at Columbia University (CASA), more than 5 million high school students (31.5 percent) admitted to binge drinking at least once a month. Even more interesting is that there is no real gender gap anymore. Both male and female ninth graders are just as likely to drink (40.2 percent of boys and 41 percent of girls) and binge drink, too (21.7 percent of boys and 20.2 percent of girls). Many adolescents use alcohol to numb the pain of depression.

In 2003, it was reported that

- 80 percent of high school students had tried alcohol.
- 70 percent of high school students had smoked cigarettes.
- 47 percent of high school students had used marijuana.

- 29 percent of high school seniors had used some other illegal drug such as Ecstasy.[3]

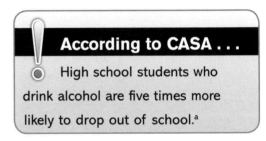

According to CASA . . .

High school students who drink alcohol are five times more likely to drop out of school.[a]

Again, these are common behaviors of adolescents trying to mask their feelings of depression, trying different substances (including prescription drugs, often prescribed to someone else) to alter their depressed moods.

Beer and other types of alcohol are implicated in the top three causes of teen deaths:[4]

1. Accidents (such as traffic fatalities and drowning)
2. Homicide
3. Suicide

Underage drinkers are at greater risk of nicotine and illegal drug addiction. Again, when using drugs such as alcohol or pot, the major feeling that remains after the effects of each drug wear off is depression.

Those who begin drinking before age fifteen are four times likelier to become alcoholics than those who do not drink before age twenty-one.[5]

The main point to remember here is that alcohol is a depressant. Young people think it makes them laugh, have fun, or blow off steam. However, drinking can lead to depressive feelings.

Substance-induced mood disorders is the diagnosis if mood changes are the direct result of substances such as drugs, alcohol, or medications, or exposure to toxins, according to psychologist Deborah Serani, who wrote *Living with Depression*.[6] Serani has suffered from depression since early childhood.

(Accidental) Medication Induced Depression

I spoke to a mother whose daughter was diagnosed with polycystic ovary disease (a disease that affects girls within the first two years of the onset of menstruation) and put on a medication to help with cysts and weight gain. The medication did what it was supposed to, at first, but gradually the daughter became more and more withdrawn and depressed. She felt she had no friends anymore and lost interest in sports, among other worrisome behaviors. Her mother was afraid she was abused in some way, or had some other trauma occur that her daughter wasn't telling her about. Several months later, the parents asked their doctor if her medication could be to blame for this change in moods, and he felt it could. She was taken off the medication, and almost forty-eight hours later, she had returned to her own positive self, the depression lifting tremendously!

Sometimes medications that are meant to help a certain disorder or disease can negatively affect moods. Care must be taken when placing young adults on any kind of medication. Teens must also keep careful watch on their emotional well-being and behaviors, as medications can have harmful side effects that take several weeks to show up. Be sure to tell a trusted adult or physician if you feel down.

Eating Disorders: Anorexia and/or Bulimia and Depression

While changes in appetite due to depression do not necessarily turn into an eating disorder, and those who have eating disorders are not always depressed, the problems of depression and eating disorders do sometimes coexist.

When so much of your life seems out of your control with your depressed mood and too many or not enough feelings, you may become vulnerable to eating disorders. It seems like one small thing in your life that you can control is *food*. Your self-worth may be tied up in your own body image. You can have a distorted view of your appearance, which unfortunately can lead to starving yourself or binging and purging, which is where a person severely overeats, then either vomits or uses laxatives to get rid of the food they've ingested. This is a medical disorder that needs serious medical attention.

Depression is the most common co-occurring psychiatric problem associated with eating disorders.[7] According to various studies, somewhere between 20 and 98 percent of eating disorder patients have been diagnosed with some sort of depression.[8] In addition, the primary mood symptom for depression in adolescents may be irritability rather than sadness.[9]

Here are some statistics on eating disorders:

- It is estimated that 8 million Americans have an eating disorder (7 million women and 1 million men).
- One in 200 American women suffers from anorexia.

"Fat. Ugly. Disgusting. That's what she sees in her reflection. She's become convinced that it's the truth. Her thoughts are poisoned with the voices of others, whispering silent judgments over and over inside her skull. She squeezes her eyes shut against them, pressing her palms to her ears, desperately trying to block them out, but it's too late; they've become a part of her."—XpurplemacaroniX, teen, excerpt from article on *TeenInk.com*[b]

- Two to three in 100 American women suffer from bulimia.
- One in five Americans suffers from mental illnesses such as mood disorders (i.e., depression, bipolar, anxiety), which can be closely related to eating disorders, either by cause or effect.
- An estimated 10–15 percent of people with anorexia or bulimia are males.[10]

When treating depression and eating disorders, a combination of medication and cognitive behavioral therapy (CBT) is often prescribed. CBT helps more in the long run, since what is learned stays with a person throughout his life. Once

Statistics on Eating Disorders and Depression

According to the National Association of Anorexia Nervosa and Associated Disorders' website,

- almost 50 percent of people with eating disorders meet the criteria for depression.
- anorexia is the third most common chronic illness among adolescents.
- 95 percent of those who have eating disorders are between the ages of twelve and twenty-five.
- eating disorders have the highest mortality rate of any mental illness.
- 86 percent report onset of an eating disorder by age twenty (43 percent report onset between ages sixteen and twenty).
- over one-half of teenage girls and nearly one-third of teenage boys use unhealthy weight control behaviors such as skipping meals, fasting, smoking cigarettes, vomiting, and taking laxatives.
- 25 percent of college-aged women engage in binging and purging as a weight-management technique.
- the mortality rate associated with anorexia nervosa is twelve times higher than the death rate associated with all causes of death for females fifteen to twenty-four years old.[c]

If you suspect you may have an eating disorder, please seek help immediately! Tell an adult you trust. You can also call your local hospital, confide in your general practitioner (doctor), or go to EatingDisordersAnonymous.org for more information.

a patient quits taking a medication, the benefits of the drug end right away. That is a possible reason that patients who go off medication tend to relapse. The bottom line is that patients have to be willing to change their behaviors, and doing so through CBT is a great start.

Eating disorders can become a way of life, if you don't get them in check, and you could suffer the consequences by having long-term health issues, including depression. Another health issue might include dental problems as a result of purging. The acid from your stomach can eat away at the backs of your teeth, thus weakening them. You can rupture your esophagus by purging too much, too fast, or too often. Sexual functioning may decrease, as well. For girls, your periods may become sporadic or stop, decreasing the ability to become pregnant. What you might think of as "just something I do to feel in control" can really become *out of* control quickly!

Cutting and Self-Injuring

Sometimes a person feels that she cannot express herself and her feelings in words, so she might turn to self-injuring, or self-harm, like cutting. Many teens who suffer from depression also self-injure themselves. Perhaps they feel they have no choice, and that it is the only way to cope with feelings like emptiness, guilt, sadness, self-loathing, or even rage, which are symptoms of depression. But the temporary relief self-harm brings doesn't last long and can cause more problems in the long run.[11] Self-injuring might also be a cry for help.

It is reported that cutting, and other forms of self-injury, release endorphins that make a person feel better. However, there are risks associated with such behaviors. There is the possibility of infection from the actual cuts, not to mention that open wounds increase the risk of serious blood contamination such as Hepatitis B, AIDS, and other diseases. Burning, picking skin, pulling hair, biting nails until they bleed, and hitting oneself are other forms of destructive, self-injuring behavior that can be dangerous.

Hollywood Explores Cutting in *28 Days*

In the movie *28 Days*, released in 2000, Sandra Bullock's character is sent to mandatory drug rehab for drunk driving. She discovers her roommate cutting herself. When she asks her why she does it, the roommate replies, "It makes me feel better."

"Than what?!" Bullock asks.

"Everything else," the roommate says.

There are also the emotional scars the physical ones leave as reminders. The cuts on your arms or legs, which people can see, comment on, or question, can be detrimental to your well-being. Perhaps you don't mind the attention that the scars bring, but other times they may make you feel self-conscious and, in turn, weak or worthless.

Why Would People Intentionally Self-Injure or Self-Harm If It's Bad for Them?

According to HelpGuide.org, there are several ways a depressed person feels it can help. It helps express feelings that can't be put into words, releases the pain

What Does *Self-Harm* Mean?

Self-harm or self-injury is intentionally doing something to hurt yourself. Examples of such behavior include the following:

- Scratching your skin severely
- Cutting yourself
- Burning or scalding yourself
- Hitting yourself or banging your head
- Punching things or throwing your body against walls and hard objects
- Sticking objects into your skin
- Intentionally preventing wounds from healing
- Swallowing poisonous substances or inappropriate objects
- Driving recklessly
- Binge drinking
- Taking too many drugs
- Having unsafe sex[d]

If you do any of these things to yourself, you should evaluate your behavior and see if it has become a habit. It could become an addictive pattern. In the end, it can make you feel worse about yourself or, in extreme cases, lead to major depression or even suicide.

and tension the depressed person feels inside, helps him feel in control, distracts him from overwhelming emotions or difficult life circumstances, relieves guilt by punishing himself, and makes him feel alive, or just feel *something*, instead of feeling numb.[12]

What Are Some Warning Signs to Look Out for If I Feel Someone I Know Might Be Self-Harming?

- Scars and wounds that are unexplained or seem to be a series of "accidental" injuries
- Blood stains on clothing, towels, bedding, or tissues
- Unexplained injuries by someone who is "overly clumsy"
- Covering up with clothing, often wearing long sleeves and/or long pants, even in warm weather
- Isolating oneself for long periods of time
- Irritability[13]

It might be hard for you to confront a friend or family member, and you don't want her to feel attacked or on the defensive, so try not to overreact. Although you may be afraid for the person, not understand, or even feel angry, do your best not to show all of your feelings right away. Reveal them slowly together, so the person who is self-injuring feels she can trust you and tell you how she feels and what is going on with her.

I Recognize Myself When Reading This Section on Self-Injury. Where Can I Go for Help?

While friends and family can be supportive if you open up to them, they aren't necessarily going to be able to help you stop such behaviors. You may want to begin by reaching out to a trusted adult such as a teacher, coach, neighbor, youth officer, mentor, or religious person in your life such as a priest or rabbi. Once you feel more accepting of the idea that you need help, you can try to find a counselor, therapist, or psychiatrist. (If you are a minor, under eighteen years of age, you will probably need a guardian's permission for treatment.) Here are two places to turn to immediately if you feel you are out of control:

- S.A.F.E. Alternatives info line (U.S.), 800-366-8288, for referrals and support for self-harm, or cutting
- National Suicide Prevention Lifeline (U.S.), 800-273-8255, if you are in crisis and are having suicidal thoughts

Trichotillomania

What is it? Trichotillomania is when a person repetitively and uncontrollably pulls out her hair, eyelashes, or eyebrows. This is a condition separate from obsessive-compulsive disorder, Tourette's syndrome, and pervasive developmental disorder (infantile autism).

People who have this habit feel a sense of relief or pleasure when pulling out hair. They may even have a sense of tension before doing it or when trying to resist the urge.

While this isn't necessarily a direct consequence of depression, it can be associated with mood or anxiety disorders, and feelings of depression are also very common.[14]

Hoarding: Obsessive-Compulsive Hoarding Disorder

When you surround yourself with things, you could be trying to fill a void that is unfillable. It can even get out of control. It is a condition known as hoarding.

Internet Chat Rooms: Friend or Foe?

While doing research for this book, I crept around some various depression chat rooms online. I can't say that I found any of them helpful. A lot of times I read posts about people having action plans to harm themselves. I feel like some members were just telling people that it is OK to do harmful behaviors, or that they were giving other people who are in a vulnerable state ideas about bad things to do to themselves.

Occasionally, I'd read something helpful like ideas to cope with depression, but that was rare. Chat rooms were not some uplifting place, as I had hoped they would be, and often made me feel worse, not better, when reading posts.

I found it worsened my depressive moods. One young woman (Veronica, early twenties) felt similarly about online websites and chat rooms, saying in a face-to-face interview with me, "A lot of websites that deal with depression just make me [feel] more sad. I mean, it's nice to not feel alone, but it doesn't help *me* to surround myself with depressed thoughts [that are expressed on these sites]."[e]

> ! **Why Do Some Teens Hoard?**
>
> There can be many reasons why someone hoards. Some of them might include having difficulty making decisions, the inability to categorize items and find a proper "space" for them in one's home, and finding it difficult to give a clear value to an object.[f]
>
> More research needs to be done on hoarding to determine whether it is part of obsessive-compulsive disorder, which can be prevalent in a family and therefore genetic, or whether it is a learned behavior, or the combination of both.[g]

That's not to say all teens who hoard are depressed, or that all depressed people hoard. However, these two conditions can sometimes coexist, and hoarding could be exacerbated by depression.

In addition to the dangerous conditions that could arise from hoarding, such as bugs, mice, and black mold, it is not a good habit for your psyche. There are television shows that explore the disorder, how professional organizers are called in to help clean up the physical mess, and then follow-ups on how the people who hoard are recovering. The disorder is something that needs to be handled with psychotherapy, in most cases.

So what can you do if you find yourself unable to get rid of the simplest of things, including wrappers or other garbage, all the way to collecting way too many things, such as Beanie Babies or fast food toys? To be honest, you have to see it as a problem and/or want to change the behavior yourself. (Many hoarders don't seem to mind their living conditions. It is usually a friend or relative that seeks help for the hoarder.) If you, yourself, don't view it as a problem, you may refuse help or drop out of a treatment program.

If you *do* see your hoarding behavior and tendencies as becoming out of control, you can try CBT or behavior therapy with a licensed professional.[15] You *can* get better. You just have to be willing to put in the effort and have the belief that you can do it!

Running Away from Home When Depressed

If your home life feels less than ideal, makes you feel depressed, or is outright dangerous, you might be contemplating running away from home. Please reconsider! There are many predators out there that take advantage of young people out on their own without any adult supervision or protection. Not only could you fall prey to sex trafficking, where you could be kidnapped and forced to prostitute yourself, essentially being sold into sexual slavery—an example is what happened to the daughter in the 2008 movie *Taken*, with Liam Neeson—but you could be sexually abused, mugged, or killed. There are other options that you might consider before doing the extreme act of running away from home.

To begin, you need to find an adult you respect and trust to help you. If there is abuse, such as emotional, physical, sexual, or drug abuse in your home, it is definitely a place you need to clear out of. (Note: I'm talking about real abuse here, not simply a parent having high expectations for you and setting limits, or being overly strict.) When abused, you may be scared and not know where to turn. This abuse could trigger a depressive episode. That's why you'll need the help of an adult.

First, consider possible other places you'd feel safe living, such as with a relative, like an aunt, uncle, cousin, or even grandparent. Your abusive parent might not like this, and might put up a real fight. In order for your wishes to be considered, there would have to be proof that your living conditions are unsafe for you. You would have to report any abuse to a teacher or police or some other authority figure. It would have to be documented. There are laws and places such as the Department of Children and Family Services, that keep children (minors under eighteen years old) safe in the home.

Best-case scenario, your family could participate in counseling and develop positive solutions together. Perhaps you could talk to your parent(s) about staying at a friend's or relative's house temporarily until you are able to gather your thoughts and things calm down around your house. This suggestion helps a teen who is just having the normal growing pains of living with a parent and feeling misunderstood, unappreciated, or annoyed in general with the relationship as it stands (which is totally natural, given your age).

In the most extreme case, and as a last-ditch effort/final option after going through counseling as a family, you could always consider emancipating yourself from your parent or legal guardian, if you are sixteen years old or older. This is a very difficult choice that will not only be expensive, but a legal battle for you to face as well. I would only consider this if you have tried all other alternatives.

No matter what your reasoning, whether it is abuse, neglect, or mild edginess, do *not* consider running away as a viable option. Seek help from a trusted adult first, please!

Withdrawing from People and Activities (Isolating)

When you're feeling depressed, you don't always want to deal with your life and/ or the people in it! Maybe you just don't know how to solve your problems in certain situations or relationships. However, mentally and physically checking out is simply not the healthiest option for how to deal with your depression. Isolating will only intensify your depressive feelings. Relationships and activities that you participate in could *help* you through this trying time, and pushing everyone else away just further isolates you and compounds your depression. Seek help!

It's difficult for caretakers (family, friends, relatives, etc.) to simply step back and watch you pull away from people who have meant something to you in the past . . . especially if *they* are some of the ones you are pulling away from. Your parents, for example, may want to help you more than anyone else. They are your primary caretakers and have been your whole life. Ideally, in most cases, their concern for you is genuine, and when they offer to help, take them up on it. Be inquisitive; ask what they think you should do, or what they had in mind when suggesting you "get help." Chances are they might be feeling as helpless as you are now, but if you can brainstorm together and *consider* solutions like therapy with a counselor or psychiatrist, medication, or even hospitalization, you might just find the treatment that works best for you and your entire family.

Untitled

Look behind the smile
Those pearly whites
That hide everything
The pain
The fear
The absence
Never knowing where to turn
Which path will cause me
To crash and burn
But you'll never know
You'll never see
Behind these pearly whites
Protecting me
Do you really want
To see
The real me?
—Christina, age 17[16]

Promiscuity

Do the clothes you wear say what you want about yourself? Perhaps you're dressing more provocatively to gain attention. Have you sent risqué pictures of yourself to someone, or been sexting with that person?

When you feel sad or alone, sometimes an intimate connection such as sex seems like a good idea for helping you feel more alive or part of something greater than yourself. You must first consider, however, that there are health risks to having sex or even multiple sexual partners, especially if you don't take precautions against STDs (sexually transmitted diseases) and use contraception to prevent pregnancy.

Have you had sex with several people, only to find you're more lonely and depressed than before? It is a possibility. Sex without love can be very depressing and leave you feeling empty, give you low self-worth, and even lead to self-loathing. You could begin to feel self-conscious about rumors going around school about you, or experience other such stresses that can just add to your depression.

If you crave intimacy, start slow and build a relationship from scratch. Don't just skip all the preliminary steps that create a bond that can eventually lead to sex. If you are pushing people away who care for you and having casual sex to fill a void, it could backfire on you. To deal with your depression, you might want to take sex out of the equation altogether until you can sort out your feelings and get your emotional well-being more stabilized.

Prostitution

One of the riskiest behaviors teens, or even adults, can participate in is prostitution. Not only is it illegal, but the health risks alone far outweigh the benefits. Perhaps you fell into prostitution and fear there is no way out. In some cases, that could be true, for the moment. However, there are places you can go to try and break the cycle and get away from your situation. Read on . . .

Children of the Night

A woman named Lois Lee was a graduate student working at UCLA (University of California, Los Angeles) in the 1970s, studying sociology. She has since spent her time advocating for prostitutes to help them get out of "the life." She was especially interested in helping underage hookers who were in most need of help. In the past, some children prostitutes were locked up in detention centers, but today they are living on the streets instead, without any adult to provide for them. If they *did* turn to prostitution, it made them ineligible to live in foster homes. "They were falling between the cracks," said Lee to Kimberly Sevcik, reporter for *Good* magazine. "There were no social services available to them."[17] Whether it's before or after turning to a life of prostitution, mood disorders such as depression, can become more prevalent.

In 1979, Lois Lee founded Children of the Night, originally as a drop-in center. Eventually, she received large grants from well-known celebrities such as Hugh Hefner and Johnny Carson, among others. With those grants, she was able to turn Children of the Night into a live-in shelter, which she still runs as of December

2013. It is located in Los Angeles, California, and the residents have their needs met and then some! They arrive from all over the country via airplanes and cabs. They are assigned to semiprivate bedrooms and given a CD player or DVD player to use while there.

There are beauty treatments such as haircuts and manicures given by volunteers from local upscale salons. In addition, there is a fully accredited school onsite that all the girls attend. They can also attend workshops held by professional photographers, yoga experts, meditation specialists, as well as acting, screenwriting, and dance professionals.

To find out more about Children of the Night and how it might be able to help you or a friend, go to www.childrenofthenight.org. It serves eleven- to seventeen-year-olds and funds Taxi/Airfare for Shelter Intake (which means interviewing a person to see if she meets the requirements to live there) twenty-four hours a day, seven days a week. Children of the Night has a toll free hotline, 1-800-551-1300. The hotline has been running since 1979! Children and young adults do not have to be under eighteen years of age to receive comprehensive social services; the eleven-to-seventeen age requirement is only for those who want to *live* on the premises. There is a new branch in Los Angeles called Children of the Night WOW! at the same toll-free number and website. (To contribute to this nonprofit organization, search its website.)

Partying Too Much

If you've found yourself partying too much (drinking or doing drugs), it doesn't necessarily mean that you're addicted; perhaps you are trying to self-medicate. You're trying to numb your emotional pain with substances. As you may have already learned, it often makes your pain and depression worse, not to mention your overall health. Hangovers don't feel good, along with other symptoms from excessive drinking and drug use. While you might feel pleased that you're getting out there around people when all you *want* to do is pull the covers over your head and hide from the world, it isn't exactly the best way to go about jumping into socializing again. The fact that drugs and underage drinking are both illegal should be an incentive to avoid them, but the fact that they will exacerbate your depression is all the more reason to "just say no."

Smoking

Smoking is another way those with depression choose to self-medicate. "Research has suggested that something in cigarette smoke has antidepressant properties, which explains why cigarette smoking is much more common among depressed patients," according to an article at www.psychcentral.com.[18]

According to the U.S. Centers for Disease Control and Prevention, 43 percent of people over the age of twenty who suffer with depression are also smokers.[19] That number is similar to smoking rates found in the population as a whole when the U.S. Surgeon General first reported on the dangers of smoking in 1964. Although the health hazards are written clearly on the packaging of cigarettes, more than 45 million American adults still smoke![20]

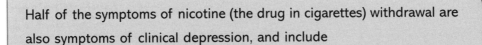

Coincidence? It's No Wonder!

Half of the symptoms of nicotine (the drug in cigarettes) withdrawal are also symptoms of clinical depression, and include

- dysphoric or depressed mood,
- insomnia,
- difficulty concentrating, and
- increased appetite or weight gain.

Then there are other symptoms of nicotine withdrawal that aren't depression related, but involve emotional struggles. They are

- irritability,
- frustration,
- anger,
- anxiety, and
- restlessness.

It's only natural that those who suffer from depression don't want to quit smoking. Quitting will cause feelings similar to those they are already struggling against. That's why some form of psychotherapy should be incorporated into any efforts to quit smoking. Behavioral therapy and talk therapy are two avenues that work well when trying to kick the habit.[h]

Smoking is a hard habit to quit. Many smokers try to quit several times, often unsuccessfully. To be successful, some have found that medications can aid in quitting. In the past, there was a commonly prescribed antidepressant sold under the name Wellbutrin given to treat depression *and* was suggested to help with smoking cessation.[21] Since quitting smoking can have side effects similar to symptoms of depression, if you're considering giving up smoking, you may want to ask your doctor if she or he thinks you could be helped by medication. Another smoking cessation medication is Bupropion (Zyban) which can be an effective antidepressant.[22] If your doctor feels this could be beneficial to you, you might be helping two problems (smoking and depression) with one medication. It is not a certainty that you would be helped, but definitely worth asking about!

Risky Behaviors, Negative Peer Groups, and Impulsivity

When people are depressed, their will to live can, at times, be in question. That's why they may choose to participate in activities that the average person would not consider being involved in. Some of these activities include

- stealing/shoplifting,
- burglary,
- vandalism,
- joining a gang or other negative peer group,
- playing "chicken" with a train or an oncoming car, and
- driving recklessly or breaking rules just because.

Maybe you haven't joined a gang, but you've started hanging out with friends that are real risk takers. They like to pressure you into daring activities that put you (or others) in harm's way. Things that seem silly and like a game, such as playing chicken with a car or a train, are huge decisions that you can't take back. It might be stated as "showing your bravery" when, in fact, it's simply a stupid decision. You don't need to prove yourself to anyone who pretends to be a real

"Morality is thinking of others as well as yourself. It's learning what other people need and trying to give it to them. The opposite of morality is thinking only of yourself, or doing whatever suits you or whatever you can get away with… morality helps you feel you're a good person."—the editors of *Struggle to Be Strong: True Stories by Teens about Overcoming Tough Times*[i]

friend. *Real* friends don't do things like that to each other. Hanging out with a crowd of risk takers, for example, can be just as dangerous to your mental health. Plus, these activities could lead to things you may not have thought of, such as doing jail time, lifelong medical conditions such as paralysis, or even serious harm to others.

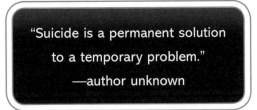

"Suicide is a permanent solution to a temporary problem."
—author unknown

If you're having trouble with your family, school, or work, you might fall in with a gang. Members might promise love, support, and "family" that you don't feel you have right now. In truth, you will be asked to give much more than you get. You will compromise your safety, maybe the safety of others, and your well-being by taking part in unlawful acts.

Harm to Others

Sometimes people with depression want to harm others. They feel so horrible themselves that they just want to spread their pain. This might include harming animals and go as far as hurting others. A teenager might provoke fights, take part in cyberbullying, or bully someone in person. With school shootings in the news, you can see that people don't always contain the depression, anger, and hopelessness in their lives. This is an extreme example, but one to be aware of, too.

Suicide

If you find yourself feeling like, "Who cares? What do I have to lose?" please reevaluate your situation.

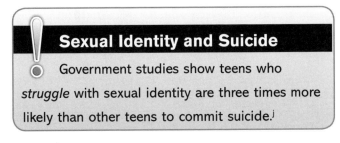

Sexual Identity and Suicide

Government studies show teens who *struggle* with sexual identity are three times more likely than other teens to commit suicide.[j]

When you are young, you may not fully comprehend the finality of death. You could be romanticizing your funeral with people milling around, crying for you. This might give you a feeling of importance and comfort. However, the cold, hard fact is that you will be gone forever. Forever. You won't be enjoying the things you once enjoyed—the conversations with friends, hanging out with your peers, even attending school. Times are tough for you at the moment. Perhaps the world seems dismal, and not even worth being here for. However, these are temporary feelings. It may not seem like it, but that is a certainty of life. Things change. There will be joy again. Just hang in there.

Suicidal thoughts can come for a variety of reasons, and they aren't always for the drastic reasons one might imagine. Suicide is many times related to a situation, and that often entails a loss. According to clinical psychotherapist Debra Koenitz, LCPC, ATR-BC, there are usually three steps a person goes through when going down that dark path. Often some sort of depressive feelings are at the root of the trigger that causes suicidal thoughts or feelings.

1. Passive thoughts: *The person thinks, "I want the situation to end."* This negative thought process can be helped with interventions such as CBT, solution-focused therapy, expression therapies, affirmations, or counseling.

Warning of Suicide Risk in Children and Teens on Medication

Medication, such as antidepressants, may start making someone feel better in as little as one to three weeks; but it could take as long as six to eight weeks to have a noticeable improvement.

However, if you as a child or a teen are on antidepressants, you *must* be monitored carefully. An adult needs to look for warning signs that could indicate a suicidal risk, especially in the first few weeks of taking any medication. That adult should keep in constant contact with the physician who has prescribed the appropriate drug to you.

While it may take a few weeks for an antidepressant to start making a marked improvement, those first few weeks could exacerbate the problem, increasing the risk of children or teens thinking about or attempting suicide. Common warning signs could include

- talking, drawing, or writing about death;
- giving away belongings;
- withdrawing from family and friends;
- having a way to commit suicide available;
- engaging in copycat behaviors.[k]

As a teen, be aware of such risks, and remember to discuss all options with your doctor before beginning any medications to manage your depression!

2. Developing a plan: *The person has a way to end his or her life.* These thoughts can be extinguished by counseling, communicating with a support network, or removing items that could lead to an actual suicide plan (removing pills, guns, etc., that could enable a plan to be acted out).

3. Deciding to act: *The person might have tunnel vision at this point and not be able to see other options besides suicide.* Better options would be reaching out for immediate help, such as calling a support line, going to the emergency room or an inpatient hospital for mental disorders, or calling 9-1-1.[23]

Lesbian, Gay, and Bisexual Youth Study Regarding Suicide

According to a study conducted in Oregon as part of the "Oregon Healthy Teens Survey" from 2006 to 2008, researchers wanted to see if social environment

My First Major Depressive Episode

An anonymous interviewee looks back:

The summer between freshman and sophomore year of high school, there was an accident and two boys I knew got too far out on a huge lake [Lake Michigan] on a small boat, and must have tried to swim back to shore. They both drowned. It was my first experience with death of someone my age. I was so devastated!

A few weeks later, my great aunt died. Then my first childhood crush was diagnosed with leukemia. The combination of the three events was way too much for me to handle. I decided that I would rather die than go to another funeral. I became obsessed with death, and how it would be easier to join them than to remain among the living. I never sought out counseling or told my parents about my feelings.

I left school one afternoon, convinced to end my life. I had a plan. After I left the school, I kept walking and walking (school was several miles from home) and ended up at a church. I sat there for hours and just prayed for the strength to go on, and not end my life. I knew it was wrong to kill yourself, but I felt the world would not notice if I wasn't there. My parents had lots of kids, so I thought they'd just get over it. I'm thankful that I had a strong religious upbringing and that sitting alone in a church with my own thoughts kept me from committing suicide. That action would have been a huge mistake. There is so much in life I would have missed, so I'm grateful to still be here.[1]

Charlene's Story

When you think of a person considering ending his or her life, you think of something monumental triggering that idea, such as dealing with the death of a loved one, or failing out of school. But that is not always the case. Something as seemingly innocent as being overweight can bring a person to think of harming herself, as you will see from seventeen-year-old Charlene Johnson's example:

"I was feeling fat and ugly, and thought I had no reason to live if I looked this way," Charlene says. "At first I used to just lie in bed and cry myself to sleep. I'd have horrible dreams about death and how bleak the future would be if I decided to stay alive. . . . Things seemed so weird to me. I didn't want to do anything but stay in my room and cry. Sometimes I'd write poems about the way I was feeling, but that only made me more depressed. I realized I was getting worse. I knew I needed some kind of help."

Charlene's cry for help was a suicide note to her twin sister. She had gathered up all the pills she could find around her house and hidden them under her pillow. Her sister shared the note with their foster mother, who came and immediately asked her why she would think of doing something so horrible. Her foster mother then told her that if she did succeed in killing herself, she'd be taking a lot of people with her. She held Charlene in her arms and cried, telling her never to think about killing herself again, and then got her some help from a therapist.

Charlene said, "I hadn't been thinking about the people in my life. I hadn't realized I wouldn't be hurting myself as much as I would hurt the people who loved me."[m]

This is a huge realization that most suicidal people really don't comprehend. There *are* people who love you, whose lives will be affected forever if you are no longer here. Some peoples' lives you've touched, you may never even realize!

mattered in likelihood of suicide attempts, while taking into consideration other individual-level risk factors (such as depression, binge drinking, peer victimization, physical abuse by adults). The results showed that among lesbian, gay, and bisexual youth, the risk of attempting suicide was 20 percent greater in unsupportive environments compared to supportive environments.[24] That leads to the

Statistics on Suicide

In 2007, suicide was the third leading cause of death among people between the ages of fifteen and twenty-four in the United States. Suicide and suicidal behavior are not normal responses to stress. Lots of people have stress but are not suicidal.[n]

Research shows that the risk for suicide is associated with changes in brain chemicals called neurotransmitters, including serotonin. Decreased levels of serotonin have been found in people with depression, impulsive disorders, and a history of suicide attempts, and in the brains of suicide victims.[o]

- Adolescents ages fifteen to nineteen had 6.9 suicide deaths per 100,000 teens that age.[p]
- Young adults ages twenty to twenty-four had 12.7 suicide deaths per 100,000 people that age.[q]
- Nearly five times as many males as females ages fifteen to nineteen died by suicide.[r]

conclusion that the social environment surrounding these teens greatly affects suicidal tendencies over and above the other individual-level risk factors mentioned earlier.[25]

Loss

Other things that trigger suicidal thoughts can be huge life hurdles such as death of a loved one, or even an acquaintance, when you're young. If, let's say, a classmate dies . . . you may not have known that person well, or been friends, but the shock and loss of losing someone that you "actually knew" can be devastating!

Perhaps you're dealing with the loss of a parent, a sibling, a pet, or even the loss of a relationship—a friendship, or a romantic interest. Loss is difficult at every age, but in the teen years, it is especially difficult to process. Many teens are so "in the present" that they cannot see themselves in five or ten years, when their lives will be dramatically different. Imagine how different things could be in ten years! You could be through with school, have your own apartment, have a career, or maybe even have a family. Think of all the things you would be willing

A TED Talk on Mental Illness, Depression, and Suicide

The website TED.com is filled with speeches of various lengths, on nearly any topic you can think of. In April 2013, a speech on mental illness, depression, and suicide was added to the website. The speaker provided graphs and slides showing how the number of suicides has not decreased over the years, in comparison to the decreased numbers of deaths from other diseases such as cancer, stroke, and heart attacks. National attention must be focused on mental illness to help bring down the number of people who suffer and die by suicide.

You can watch the TED speech given by Thomas Insel, director of the National Institute of Mental Health, on the Internet by going to http://www.ted.com/talks/thomas_insel_toward_a_new_understanding_of_mental_illness.html (accessed December 17, 2013).

to give up if you gave into the dark thoughts of suicide. What a horrible waste! Please give serious thought to alternatives.

Reaching out for help with your depression can be as simple as checking this very book out from the library; it could be the first step to realizing you have a problem that may very well be out of your control. Depending on your depression's length and severity, you might need professional help such as counseling or even medication, both of which will be discussed in future chapters.

Suicide is never an option to get out of a bad situation; it is simply a poor decision made in a moment when you're not thinking with your best self. Please take it out of your repertoire of possible solutions now and forever.

When a Friend Confides Suicidal Thoughts to You

Friends don't tell on other friends. Isn't that the "code" of real friends? No! Not always. If a friend is struggling and in a truly dark place, there's only so much you can do by being a good listener. The fact is he or she may need more serious help. You're a teen yourself, not a professional. Are you someone people always confide in? That is too much for one person to bear. Sure you can empathize and listen when the friend is venting about what is wrong with her life. But when it

> ## Veronica's Story: Remembering a Friend
>
> When in her early teens, Veronica felt she could not confide in an adult about her depressed feelings. "I felt silly, weak, and it seemed like whining," Veronica said. She *did* tell her best friend, who also had depression. "We were too young and naïve to realize how serious it was," Veronica said. "Later, my friend committed suicide. I learned it's better not to surround yourself with people that bring you down. I found a better support system, and she [the friend] did not want help. Sometimes I feel like I should have been a better friend, but I also realize that there was help available to her, but she chose not to take it."[5]

turns to real harmful thoughts or even a suicide plan, don't take on that pressure to hide her secret.

Even if she threatens to never speak to you again, so what? If she actually kills herself, you'll never speak with her again anyway. Go to a trusted adult, perhaps her parents, a teacher or coach, or even a school counselor. If that's too difficult, then how about calling an 800 number? A hotline is available to give advice, and if possible, you can also get your friend on the phone with the support line. Whatever action you take, do it fast! You don't know how much time you have. Suicide is often an act of impulse, so you may not know what will trigger your friend to actually make the attempt.

Three Important Resources

There are three great resources you can turn to if you're afraid of your own suicidal thoughts, or if a friend has confessed such thoughts to you. The American Association of Suicidology, located in Washington DC, is one resource. The phone number is 202-237-2280 and the website is www.suicidology.org.

Another helpful resource is the American Foundation for Suicide Prevention, located in New York City, whose phone number is 888-333-AFSP (2377) (which is not a crisis line) or 212-363-3500. Its website is www.afsp.org, or you can e-mail questions to inquiry@afsp.org.

Lastly, the National Suicide Prevention Lifeline has a 24/7 helpline at 800-273-TALK (8255) to help a person in a suicidal crisis or emotional distress. There are trained counselors available on the phone, and the service is free and confidential.

RELATIONSHIPS AND HOW TO PRESERVE THEM

Though depression can sometimes immobilize you socially, there are ways to manage it so you can preserve your special relationships. Friends, family members, boy- and girlfriends, teachers, coaches, mentors, coworkers, employers, and even strangers we run into at the post office or grocery store are all people we have relationships with.

Friendships

A friend is a person who is there for you through the good times and the bad. While friends are there to support you as best they can, your illness may require more help than your friends can provide. They aren't professionally trained to deal with depression. You could benefit from the help of a therapist, a counselor, a social worker, or even a psychiatrist.

Your goal is to remain connected with others and not withdraw from them. By keeping regular contact with people, you won't become isolated, which would worsen what you're experiencing.[1] There are psychological benefits to preserving relationships. Friends can become a sounding board for you, can offer helpful advice on your personal concerns, and can be more specific than some books because they know you better than any book does.[2]

Friends, however, can get worn out by the high emotional intensity and ups and downs of the drama going on in your life, whether real or imagined. Friends might get frustrated if you don't respond to their suggestions. There are limits to the advice they can offer, especially since they are, again, not specifically trained like professionals.[3] Keep in mind you need to show support to them as well, when *they* need it. It can't always be about you. That's tough sometimes, I realize, when you're in a spiral of downward thinking. But try to take a moment and look out-

Having a friend and *being* a friend!

side yourself and your circumstances to see what is going on in the world around you. When you *do* need to be heard, to quiet that negative inner voice you may be listening to, be sure to speak up; whether it's to a friend, a teacher, a trusted adult, a religious mentor, a coworker, your parents, or your therapist, please find someone to confide in!

A twenty-year-old woman named Susan talked about opening up to friends about her depression while in middle school. She said, "[My friend] Rosemarie had always been there for me, had been my biggest supporter, she was understanding, she listened and could relate to me at that time. The other girls in middle school stopped being my friends. One of them told a few people. They thought I was overreacting and faking it." As Susan got older she found that "two recent friends have been very understanding and open."[4]

When you're depressed and don't have the energy or interest in activities, your relationships with others, such as friends, might deteriorate. This can diminish your quality of life, as it can also affect your physical health.[5]

Though it is great to have that friend to confide in, you will need to decide just how much to share and when to pull back and save certain thoughts and issues for your therapist, if you have one. If you *do* decide to seek therapy, it is a must to keep in contact with your friends. You will just have to decide what healthy discussions there can be and which topics are too personal or difficult to share with a friend.[6]

Friends forever. *Photo courtesy of Heather Schwartz*

Family Members: Siblings

As an adult looking back, I don't recall ever telling my siblings how down I was feeling. I'm sure they sensed it, since they would often take me places with them and do things to cheer me up.

Sometimes people who suffer from depression can feel that no one cares about them; they think they are a burden to others, believe they don't deserve to be

"A friend once compared my having depression to being diabetic. She said that if you were diabetic and needed insulin, no one would think twice about it. So what if you need 'x' depression medication to help you to feel 'yourself,' that's okay! I still love you, and don't think any differently about you. Depression is a medical condition, and not your fault! It really helped me to put things into perspective. I appreciated her saying that. Now if other people could only be so open-minded!"—CGS, 20-something[a]

How Depression Is Kept a Secret

Due to the stigma and shame attached to depression, many people refuse to share their feelings and/or diagnosis with family, friends, and employers. In fact, the work place isn't necessarily an appropriate place to share such personal information. In a 2006 survey,

- 74 percent of patients told their families of their depression,
- 59 percent of patients told their friends,
- 21 percent shared their diagnosis with coworkers, and
- 11 percent shared their depression diagnosis with their employers.[b]

happy, and often have many thoughts racing through their heads, many of them not good thoughts.[7]

Having a sibling or other family member who suffers from depression can take a toll on the entire family. In her account of her experience with depression, Cait Irwin wrote, "During my crisis, my brother didn't get much attention, and he often felt left out. The [family therapy] session offered him a chance to have his concerns heard by an objective ear."[8] Cait spoke of her brother begrudgingly going to a therapy session; at first he refused to take part, then ended up speaking the entire hour of the session.

Family Members: Parents

Since depression can be difficult to diagnose, family members or significant others don't always know that it's going on. It's not like having a cold, where you get symptoms quickly and they're obvious, and there are well-known, common treatments available. Depressed people can feel awful for weeks or months, perhaps even years without knowing that they may have a serious condition—depression. The signs and symptoms vary from person to person. Genetics, biology, psychology, and environment are all part of the mix that makes up depression.[9] As a family member who may have missed the signs of your loved one's depression, don't feel guilty or responsible for the person not being diagnosed sooner, or at all.

Sometimes, family members aren't supportive in any way, even if you've tried to explain what you're going through. Susan, a twenty-year-old college student, explained how her family reacted to the idea of depression while growing up: "Growing up, whenever an antidepressant ad would come on TV, my mom would say, don't ever let a doctor put you on those . . . [when you get older]. I got the impression she thought depression was all in one's attitude."[10]

Susan went on to say, "Whenever I would be sad about something or my depression was acting up for no reason (at this time my mom still didn't know about the depression/didn't believe in depression) my mom would tell me to get over it or be mad that I was sad at the most inconvenient times."

Susan had reached a low point in her life, and checked herself into a psychiatric ward for in-patient care. (She was over eighteen years old.) She said the help was invaluable, especially leading to her mother's acceptance of her depression. It made it clear that Susan's depression was, in fact, real. The acknowledgment of her illness was a turning point in their relationship.

"It also allowed me to meet others my age dealing with similar matters and with the depression. [Because] I often feel so alone and detached from others, meeting peers that understood me was amazing. It taught me CBT (cognitive behavioral therapy), opposite action, and other tools to use. They [doctors] were finally able to start seeing what meds were right for me, and I was around adults who openly knew what I was going through, yet didn't treat me differently. It was the best experience of my life so far," Susan said.[11]

An eighteen-year-old named Christopher was in a juvenile detention center for some trouble he had gotten into with his mother. Part of his service required therapy. He was very reluctant to go, and certainly did not want to open up to some stranger! While he admitted that his therapist seemed like a nice woman and was very patient in waiting for him to share things with her until he felt comfortable, he was still hesitant.

"I didn't like talking about my problems. I felt I couldn't trust anybody. I had been hurt a lot by many loved ones who were supposed to be in my corner when times got rough. They let me down big-time by misusing my trust," Christopher said.[12]

As time went on, Christopher did learn to trust, and he started expressing himself better with his therapist. Slowly, he began to tell her about his problem, to see if he could trust her. His problem was that he had a lot of anger toward his mother.

He had a major falling out with her that had escalated to a physical fight, in which he was defending himself. His mother treated Christopher as she had been treated by Christopher's father, very disrespectfully and verbally abusively. The mother seemed to take out her anger toward her ex-husband on her son.

As Christopher continued on with therapy, he began to realize that what his therapist told him was true: "The first step in forgiving someone [i.e., his mother] is to really mean it from the heart." He began to see that, "everybody makes mistakes and deserves a second chance."[13]

While Christopher has anger management hurdles to overcome, therapy has helped with his progress tremendously. The family received therapy as well, which has made all the difference in their relationships. Christopher also published two pieces in a book titled *Struggle to Be Strong: True Stories by Teens about Overcoming Tough Times*, published by Free Spirit Publishing.[14]

Family Members: Extended Family (Cousins, Aunts, Uncles, Grandparents)

Sometimes you have strong ties with extended family members. Cousins, aunts, uncles, and grandparents might be a large part of your life. If this is the case, and you truly trust them, don't be afraid to confide in them. You can tell them the problems you might be experiencing with depression. If they are the people that know you best and love you the most, then trust in them with your feelings. But remember, when an aunt, uncle, or cousin gives advice, accept it graciously. While it may or may not be great advice, take it with the consideration that it was given.

Sometimes, those we love don't know *what* to say, and their advice might be something like, "Look on the bright side," or "You have so much to be grateful for." Don't take offense to the advice they have to offer. Remember they are not professionals and are simply trying to be as supportive as possible.

It is very important not to push away those you love. If your extended family has been in your life every step of the way, and you feel they are supportive of you, then by all means, keep them in your inner circle during this rough time in your life. Try your best not to lash out at the people who love you. They are learning their way through this difficult period, just like you are. Patience is key.

Romantic Relationships

Depression can have a negative effect on your romantic relationships. If you become withdrawn and don't want to be around people, distancing yourself from those you love or pushing yourself away from everyone will cause problems with your relationships.

If you don't feel comfortable enough to share what is really going on with your partner, he or she won't understand why you're acting that way. He or she might even feel you want to break up, when in fact that may not be the case. You cannot be so afraid of losing someone that you lose him or her because of the fear of being honest about your depression diagnosis.

Self-esteem and sexuality are closely connected.[15] Many depressed people turn to sex to relieve an inner emptiness. However, when it's not from an intimate relationship, but more of a casual sex standpoint, this can just exacerbate the problem of low self-worth and loneliness. Risky behavior such as partaking in

> ### ❗ Negative Side Effects on Your Romantic Life
>
> ◉ When taking some antidepressant medication, it *could* (not always, though) affect your sexual appetite or performance. This is especially true for males. SSRI (selective serotonin reuptake inhibitor) medications such as fluoxetine, sertraline, paroxetine, fluvoxine, citalopram, and escitalopram have a listed side effect of *possible* sexual dysfunction.[c] However, symptoms of depression (even if not medicated) can include loss of desire for intimacy.

casual sex, with multiple partners over time, can be a risk not only to your mental health, but to your physical well-being, too. Why risk your health and well-being unnecessarily?

On the flip side, the loss of sexual desire or intimacy is often a common sign of depression.[16] People often associate the loss of sexual appetite in their forties and fifties with aging. However, a depressed person's sexual indifference at any age—even during teen years—can be misinterpreted by his or her partner as loss of love or attraction. This might be true, but oftentimes, it is not really the case.[17] There can be many reasons why depressed people lose interest in sex. Some people feel anxiety, pessimism, fear of rejection, or other symptoms that can simply interfere with their sexual drive.[18]

Coworkers and Employers

Telling people you work with that you suffer from depression might not be a good idea. Unfortunately, due to the stigma associated with mental disorders, there is a certain prejudice people may have. Plus, it really isn't appropriate conversation for the workplace. Although there are laws in place to protect people, such as the Americans with Disabilities Act, people of various ages have lost jobs and promotions because of their depression.[19]

There are myths about people with mental illness being dangerous and untreatable.[20] While some mental illnesses can cause psychosis, or loss of contact with reality, that doesn't necessarily have to be the case with depression. In fact, having depression doesn't mean you are a danger to those around you. Often, the one in danger is you, by having negative thoughts or dangerous behaviors that pose a risk to yourself.

Depression can cause you to no longer have the energy or desire to do normal, day-to-day activities. This might cause you to drop out of school, quit a job, or

Americans with Disabilities Act

In 1990, the Americans with Disabilities Act (ADA) was passed, which prohibited any discrimination in the workplace against people who had physical or mental disabilities that resulted in them being passed over for certain jobs. This pertained to private employers, state and local governments, employment agencies, and labor unions. Also, the law impacted companies with fifteen or more employees. The ADA was put in place to protect qualified individuals with disabilities in job application procedures, hiring, firing, advancement, and compensation.[d]

To quote section 12101 of the act, "In enacting the ADA, Congress recognized that physical and mental disabilities in no way diminish a person's right to fully participate in all aspects of society, but that people with physical or mental disabilities are frequently precluded from doing so because of prejudice, antiquated attitudes, or the failure to remove societal and institutional barriers."

take a less demanding one. This lack of energy and drive might even make your relationships deteriorate.

Even if you have a part-time job, it might be hard to stay motivated. There are ideas for how to keep your spirits or drive up during your down periods. These will be discussed further in chapter 11, "Healthy Coping Mechanisms."

Educating people about mental illness is the first step in making things better for all those who suffer, especially those who suffer in silence.

SIBLINGS OF THOSE WITH DEPRESSION

What Role Do You Play?

When your sibling has any type of illness, there are certain "roles" you, as the healthy child, might play. In the book called *Sibs: The Forgotten Family Members*, authors Nancy Hull-Mast and Diane Purcell talk about several roles family members play. It is a book about addiction, but the roles are very similar to those you find in a family dealing with depression, as well.

The first role you might be trying to play is that of a *perfectionist*. You might feel the need to be as little trouble for your parents as possible. If your sibling were to have cancer or cystic fibrosis or any other disease, you might try your

When a sibling suffers from depression.

"My sister is all vintage records and thrift store sweaters, because if she does not try to be like everyone else she can never be rejected. Because not trying scares her more than failing, she runs headlong into anything that is asked of her in hopes of acceptance. In those moments I envy her strength. In those moments she pushes me away. . . . And sometimes I see her how she sees herself; the broken edged person underneath the layer of sugar coating. I see how life has pushed her down so many times her knees are perpetually scabbed and her hands callused from picking up the shattered pieces of her life. It is in these moments that I love her most. Because in these moments I realize that she is a warrior, a queen, a dandelion lost in the wind, a river divided by a rock. There are no words to describe her. She simply is."—excerpt from essay in *Teen Ink* on a sibling with depression[a]

best to fly under the radar with your parents and just stay out of their way during your sibling's medical procedures. This would help them deal with pressing issues of your sibling's illness. The same is true when there's a mental illness in the family. But the stress of being the "perfect" son or daughter can weigh heavily on your mind.

It's hard enough being a teen and getting through your own set of problems. It's nice to be able to confide in a parent when you're having trouble with school or a friend, or when you're feeling fear over something like a test or your sibling's illness. It's okay *not* to be so perfect all the time. You can let your hair down, so to speak. The tension of trying not to make any mistakes can be exhausting, and you might come off as uptight. Do people often tell you to relax? This might be a clue that you are in the perfectionist role.

Next, you may be acting like the *forgotten child*. You try to just get by life on your own. You stay out of family arguments, keep to yourself, and often get lost in the shuffle. In fact, you wonder if you went away, would anyone notice? Your self-esteem is probably at an all-time low. You don't feel loud or exciting like your brothers and sisters. Perhaps you like quiet activities like drawing or writing. You're known as shy and introverted. The problem with this role is that you wonder if your own needs are being met. You need to speak up for yourself. While a mental illness can be overwhelming for your parents and take center stage of the family dynamic most of the time, you are still an important part of the family and deserve to be noticed and cared for just like everybody else.

Perhaps you feel resentment toward your parents for all of their time, energy, and emotions being lavished on your sick sibling. You may feel like you've been

---

Jake's Story: "Before I Understood"

Jake, age twenty-five, talks about having a sister with depression:

Several years ago, when my sister first began having trouble with depression, I didn't understand it. I would get mad at her. After all, we grew up with the same parents, same opportunities, similar experiences. How come she couldn't just be happy? She was always so down.

I didn't feel neglected by my parents or that she got more attention, because I was away from home at a boarding school. But because of that, I didn't see her day-to-day life, or how sad she was becoming.

Once I began to understand about [her] depression, I felt bad . . . selfish. I didn't reach out to her in the past, because I feel I would have been hard on her not understanding what she was going through. Now I'm so proud of her motivation to do better. She has a long-term plan to take care of herself with exercise, vitamins, and meditation. She was on medication, but has been able to [eventually] wean off of it with therapy, and a doctor's supervision.

I still worry about her, but I try to reach out to her more often.[b]

---

forgotten. In your heart, you must know that's not truly the case. When focus is pulled away from you, it's got to be for a good reason. Getting your sibling through a crisis might take precedence over asking you how the prom went or if you aced your exams. Of course, you might be anxious to share what's going on in your life, but sometimes the timing isn't right. Don't despair. Just try to be honest about your feelings. Talk to your parents and let them know when you truly do need them.

Another role you might be playing is the *partier*. You like to go out to try and forget your problems at home. Maybe you've begun to abuse substances to erase the pain and confusion that you're feeling when at home. It's difficult to see your sibling suffer with depression, but watching your sibling can make you angry too. Why should he get all the attention? You might start to cut class or drop out of your after school activities to just hang out with friends, or participate in risky behaviors such as drinking, drugging, or casual sex. Your emotions get the best of you and you feel all confused inside. This is totally natural. On the one hand, you do feel sorry for your brother or sister's struggles. But on the other hand, that doesn't mean that your mom and dad need to completely check out from the rest of the family. It would help for you to seek counseling yourself to try and get a handle on your emotions so you don't end up harming yourself or your future.

Lastly, you may take the role of the *clown*. This is the person who always has a smile on her face and is constantly cracking jokes or imitating people. She'll do anything to get a laugh or lighten the mood. She might even be disruptive in class, but the teacher can't totally hide his smile, so he lets the disruptions go with only a warning. The clown is often the center of attention and gets invited to parties, but is never allowed to relinquish that role. If you even think of having a bad day or sad moment, think again. This won't fly with those around you. They expect a show 24/7. You cannot break character if you want to stay in everyone's good graces. It's a hard facade to keep up and can be exhausting, too! When you're the clown, you risk masking your feelings for so long that you, too, could become depressed.

How Do You Get Your Needs Met?

So how can you get your needs met by your parents if your sibling has something like depression? First of all, there can be a stigma with mental illness. You might feel embarrassed and not want to confide in your friends or other people about your sibling's condition. Your sibling might not even discuss his depression with you. As someone who suffered from teen depression, I know for a fact that I never had a specific conversation with any of my four siblings about my being depressed. I tried to hide it from them as best as I could. The one person I could be myself with, and cry if I needed to, was my mother. If you have just one person that you can be your true self with, then you are very lucky. Try to identify that person and let her know that she is part of your trusted support network. Let the person know you may want to confide in him your true feelings. It can be an important thing to increase your quality of life. It would be ideal if you could seek therapy for yourself, but still you need someone you can talk to on a day-to-day basis if necessary. Usually a family member is the best place to start.

Sometimes, confiding in your parents just isn't an option, or doesn't *seem* like an option to you. They may appear so overburdened with your sibling's depression that the last thing you want to do is add to their load of troubles. Can you think of another person who might be able to relate or even empathize with you? Maybe you have another sibling, in addition to the depressed one, or a cousin you're close to, or even an aunt or uncle. Have you ever tried to reach out to someone besides your parent(s)? Give it a try. It may be difficult, while trying to preserve your family's privacy, but that doesn't mean you have to completely isolate yourself. Just do your best to be yourself and not put so much pressure on yourself all the time. You can't be perfect; you are *not* responsible for everyone's happiness, or unhappiness, as the case may be, and you needn't try to bear the brunt of your sibling's depression symptoms by yourself.

Stigmatism and Keeping Depression Secret

Mental illness has historically carried a stigma. Only recently has it been suggested, but not proven, that there are biological origins to depression. There is still much debate over whether depression is due to genes. Some researchers believe that 50 percent of depression is biological, and the remaining 50 percent is from psychological or physical factors.[1]

So what do you do with your feelings of secrecy and embarrassment about a sibling or yourself? We've discussed finding someone to confide in, someone you know, but have you ever thought of consulting a professional to help deal with *your* feelings? If you don't feel comfortable seeking counseling on your own, you might want to think about finding a support group to attend. You don't need to suffer in silence.

Many public figures with depression have had siblings that have had to deal with their famous brother or sister's depression. One modern example concerns movie star Owen Wilson, who gained fame from such movies as *Marley and Me* (2008) and *Wedding Crashers* (2005). Luke Wilson, also an actor, had to deal with his brother's depression. In fact, in 2007, Owen made a suicide attempt,[2] and it was Luke who found him after he had taken an overdose of drugs and slit his wrists.[3]

In an interview with *OK!* magazine, Luke was asked about his brother's future and if he thought Owen would be okay. He broke down in tears and simply replied, "I just don't know."[4]

How to Find a Local Support Group

- Depression and Bipolar Support Alliance has support groups that you can find by going to its website at www.dbsalliance.org.
- National Alliance on Mental Illness has groups around the country. Go to www.nami.org to find out more.
- Religious organizations often have support groups; look up local churches or synagogues in your area to see what kind they run. Oftentimes, there are groups for substance abuse, cancer, and caregivers, among others. There might be ones for depression, too. Google "Local Support Groups: Depression" to see what comes up.

As of early 2013, Owen Wilson seemed to be recovering from his illness. He has made over thirteen movies since 2007, with several other films in various stages of production. He has also worked in television since 2007. His recovery seems to be successful, if judged by his professional accomplishments, since his suicide attempt.

Dealing with Resentment toward a Sibling Living with Depression

Do you ever feel mad at your sibling for being sick and having depression symptoms? It's only natural. Don't add guilt to the list of burdens you are carrying. Perhaps you feel like she is so self-centered, only worrying about herself and how she's feeling at any given moment. Your sibling could be so absorbed in his deep, dark depression that he rarely seems to consider how *you* may be feeling.

When depressed people are in a downward spiral, they're struggling to stay afloat. It may be more than they can do to worry about you or how you're feeling. Getting through each day alive might consume their every thought. Try to imagine how that might feel.

Do you ever ask your sibling how she is feeling? Might it be possible to ask her point blank, "How are you feeling at this moment? Can I help in any way?" Depending on the reaction, you could press further by asking for help in getting her to open up. Saying something like, "I am so worried about you, and it consumes me. I want to be here for you, but sometimes I have to take care of myself, too." This is a way to tell your brother or sister that you care, but that you might need caring for, as well. Keeping the lines of communication open is one way to help dissipate your resentment toward your sibling.

Rob's Story: Finding Hope Thanks to Brother's Advice

Rob is a teen whose brother noticed that his behavior had changed and immediately suggested that Rob see a doctor. Rob did and learned that depression is a real illness that can't be fixed by being told to just "cheer up." He was told the most effective treatment would come from a doctor or other health care professional. So he began seeing a therapist, who helped him talk through his problems.

"This treatment helps me control depression in my everyday life," Rob said. "It has taken some time, but I'm finally feeling like myself again."[c]

Your Own Troubles at School

Have you found yourself getting into trouble at school? Is this a way you are silently asking for help or attention you so desperately seek? There are better ways to go about doing that. Perhaps you are simply having trouble, but not on purpose. If this is the case, you should tell your parents. Maybe you need a tutor to help with your grades. Maybe you need to talk to the school counselor to help you process your feelings, emotions, even fears about what is going on at home. The point is that you will need to reach out to someone, preferably an adult. Reach out to someone who can help you with what *you're* dealing with. Don't suffer in silence because you feel your problems pale in comparison to those of your sibling.

Your Goals: "What about Me?"

It's important to keep moving forward, no matter what your situation is at home. If your brother or sister is having trouble getting through day-to-day life, and you feel like you're holding your breath, fearing something bad might happen (like a suicide attempt), try to focus on the things you can control . . . like your future. What are you passionate about? What do you want to do when you grow up? Are you going to go away to college? Do you have a job? Focus on your goals and what you can do to achieve them.

It's hard not to get sucked into your sibling's mental illness sometimes. You might want to always be there for him. Do you call him or text him several times a day? Do you hang out with her whenever she will let you? While this is all well and good, you don't want it to steal the focus from your life and your goals. You cannot become codependent on your sibling's moods. Codependency means you allow your moods and feelings to depend on how another person is feeling. You are psychologically dependent on his or her mental state. There are support groups to help you if you feel you have become codependent on someone. Go to the Co-Dependents Anonymous website (www.coda.org) to learn more.

Here's a list of eight things some adults might want you to do for yourself, suggested by Anne Courtright in *Reaching Your Goals: The Ultimate Teen Guide:*

1. Get a job.
2. Buy your own car.
3. Pay for your own car insurance.
4. Get better grades in school.
5. Go to college.
6. Join a religious youth group.

7. Train to become a professional athlete.
8. Enlist in the military.[5]

Some of these might appeal to you, while others may not. That's okay. Give some of them a try and see where they take you.

Are there certain talents you have that you may not have explored? Perhaps you could enter a writing contest, participate in an art show, or audition for a play. You could do something as simple as taking a dance class, a photography class, or even a ceramics class. The arts are a wonderfully creative outlet that can be a cathartic experience and not only give you joy and a sense of accomplishment, but bring joy to others as well. The time to focus on yourself is now. Go out there and do something special!

WHEN A PARENT HAS DEPRESSION

....

Discovering Your Loved One's Depression: How Did It Happen?

Was there an event or situation that let you know your parent was having trouble with depression? It could be something like your mother or father staying in bed for several days in a row, all the way to a suicide attempt. As you learned in chapter 1 on warning signs and symptoms, detecting someone's depression might not be as easy as you think. How do you tell if someone is just feeling down or if it's something more serious like clinical depression?

Let's review the technical differences. Being clinically depressed means having symptoms that often last for more than two weeks. The length and severity of the symptoms are what differentiate sadness from clinical depression.

Perhaps you noticed medication in your parent's bathroom. Did you ask him what he was taking and why? Perhaps he is on antianxiety and/or antidepression medication. Sometimes it's hard to ask the difficult questions. And perhaps your parent is willing to be honest with you, or perhaps he'd like to remain private. What's important is what matters to you. Do her moods affect you and your daily life? Does she embarrass you by showing symptoms such as not showering, not changing her clothes, or leaving the house in total disarray? Or perhaps he ignores you, or causes you to have low self-worth when he is moody or irritable, or makes you feel depressed yourself? If a parent's condition affects you directly, then you might need to have an open and honest discussion with your mother or father. It might be as easy as saying, "I'm hurting seeing you like this," or as difficult as needing to hold an intervention.

Concerns about Depression Being Hereditary

The scariest part of seeing a biological family member (i.e., parent, grandparent, aunt, uncle, cousin, sibling) suffer from depression might be wondering, "Could

When someone you love is hurting.

I have it too?" Studies have shown that the origins of depression can be caused by a mixture of genetics and other things such as stress.[1] The levels of the hormone serotonin play a large role in our brain chemistry. Serotonin has a major effect on emotions, thinking, and behavior. In a 2010 analysis of fifty-four studies dating from 2001 to 2010, which involved almost 41,000 participants, serotonin association with depression was confirmed.[2]

If you're afraid that your parent might be suffering and not seeking treatment, it is important to speak up. Whether you confront him or her, or a trusted adult, it is important to tell someone! Mental health and psychiatric disorders are serious conditions if left undiagnosed and untreated. Although there is still a stigma

What Is an Intervention?

An intervention is held to get a person who has been engaging in self-destructive behavior to see what he is doing and how it affects those around him. The goal is to get him professional help. It is usually done by a small group of people who know the person well. It can be family and friends who hold the intervention. Usually a professional counselor or mediator is there to help in the process so it can be done in a loving and caring way. Interventions are often done when people have substance abuse issues or eating disorders, or may be harming themselves or others and are not functioning well.[a]

"I've done research on bipolar disorder and believe that my brother, sister, and I have a 1 in 6 chance of having bipolar, too, since our father has it. I try to monitor all three of us to see if I see any symptoms."—William, age 19[b]

associated with mental health disorders, you don't want to risk serious side effects of depression, the worst of which are suicidal or homicidal thoughts or actions.

It is a huge undertaking when you're a teen and you see someone in your family you love not functioning well, or feeling helpless or hopeless, especially if you're afraid that your parent (or other family member) might harm herself. After all, she is supposed to be the one taking care of *you*, not the other way around. However, sometimes she just can't help it, if she's ill. This isn't a burden for you to take on alone. You must have someone available to help you help your parent. You might consider talking to another adult (like your other parent, grandparent, etc.) about options such as the aforementioned intervention.

How Friends Treat You Because of a Family Member's Depression

Have you noticed that you're always hanging out with friends at their homes? Perhaps no one ever seems to come hang out at your house. Does that bother

Resources for Family Members and Friends

There are several great resources to find further information about depression and other mood disorders available on the World Wide Web. Some of those websites are as follows:

Depression Facts—www.aboutdepressionfacts.com

HelpGuide.org—www.helpguide.org/mental/depression_teen.htm (guide for parents); www.helpguide.org/mental/depression_teen_teenagers.htm (guide for teens)

Mood Disorders Association of Ontario—www.mooddisorders.ca

National Institute of Mental Health—www.nimh.nih.gov/health/publications/depression-and-high-school-students/depression-and-high-school-students.shtml

The website of the National Institute of Mental Health (www.nimh.nih.gov) has a wealth of information about depression for everyone, from children to adults.

you? Has your home become an awkward place where your friends don't want to be around? Maybe, you're the one who doesn't want people over because you are embarrassed about your parent's behavior or other family members who are depressed. Perhaps they are moody, tearful, irritable, or are simply flat and unresponsive. For example, is your dad often despondent or disheveled, looking unkempt and kind of zoning out most of the time? Why can't he be the fun parent like those of your friends? I'm sure this isn't something your mom or dad wishes for. The awkwardness can make you feel upset.

When a parent, grandparent, or stepparent, for example, is in a deep depression, sometimes he can't just "fake it" to be all happy-go-lucky when people are around. Some depressed people are able to hide their illness and act like everything is okay, while others are just so overwhelmed that they turn inward and dismiss others around them. It is common for depressed people to physically isolate themselves from others. This can be irritating to you, and you might have mean thoughts like "Why can't my dad just be normal?" or "He should just look at all the good things we have going for us as a family and be grateful." That is often easier said than done. In fact, if you ask a depressed person what is one of the most difficult hurdles of his depression, he might say, "How others react to my moods" and also, "Feeling helpless and hopeless about my symptoms chang-

> "When my Mom is depressed, she sleeps a lot. I know she is feeling down, but I can't seem to do anything to cheer her up, and it makes me feel bad."
> —Hannah, age 15[c]

ing." It is such a difficult thing to be depressed. Unless you're going through it yourself, you really have no idea how awful it feels.

Positive Ways for You to Cope When Family Members Are Down

An important thing to realize about your parent's depression is that you do not have the power to control his or her moods. You can't be held responsible for his or her good moods or bad moods. It is out of your control. So feeling bad about it won't help. Try to simply take care of yourself and the things you *can* control, like how you are aware of and respond to your environment. Maybe you can go out with friends, try journaling, do artwork, watch a funny movie, read a book, or go exercise. Do something for yourself to keep your own moods from going down. A feeling of powerlessness is depressing in itself. Don't feed into that.

The Pressure to Be Perfect for Parents

You might feel that your actions have a great power over your parent or other family member's mood. While it is helpful to have a neat room, do well in school, and have a happy and healthy social life, these things are not going to make a bit of difference to your parent's (family member's) depression. So stop trying to be so perfect. If you are able to do these things for your own well-being, then great. But don't try to do these things to improve your parent's depression. It doesn't work that way. Just like if you get into trouble, it won't necessarily make a parent's depression worse. Your mother feels bad because she feels bad; it is simply a symptom of her own depression. It isn't hinging on your every mood. It would be nice if it was that easy, but it simply isn't. Do your best to get through life by being the best person you can be. Take care of yourself and how you're feeling on a day-to-day basis. Make healthy choices. The only person you can control is yourself. Period.

Stigma and Keeping Depression Secret

Your parent, grandparent, or stepparent's mental illness might be a horrible secret that you've been keeping, or have been told to keep quiet about by other family members. The words *mental illness* can be scary and embarrassing all at the same time. Maybe you feel bad for the things you are thinking, like "Why can't my mom just be normal?" Unfortunately, this is *normal* for her while she is depressed. Until she is able to realize there is a problem and seek help, things are not going to change. You may not want to talk with her about this, because you'll think it will make her feel worse or you'll feel like you're being confrontational, but how else will she seek the help she needs. Secrets can be hurtful for all involved. You need to realize that depression is a medical condition and no one is to blame—not you, not her, not your other family members. It is a condition like any other with medical roots. While it's not your secret to share with the world, it does affect *your* world, and you have the right to seek help for yourself. Hiding the fact of illness won't make it go away.

There is an organization called the National Alliance of Mental Illness (NAMI) that you might be able to turn to. It has a Family-to-Family Education Program available to help you learn, understand, and cope with a family member's mental illness. It helps entire families deal with the daily struggles of things like depression, and gives family members the proper tools to help work through difficult and sometimes traumatic events. To learn more, go to www.nami.org, or call 800-950-NAMI.

Dealing with Resentment toward an Ill Parent

Have you ever had the thought "I really hate my mom (grandma, stepmother, etc.) for being sick," then felt really guilty about those thoughts? It's natural. You know, in your heart, she isn't sick on purpose and it is out of her control. But perhaps you feel like she could get help if she would just ask for it. That part is true. But seeking help is a difficult task. Not only does the person need to acknowledge there is a problem, but he or she has to feel bad enough to do something about it. It's like a person who is an alcoholic, for example; he might feel like he is in control of the situation and can quit any time he wants to. For depressed people, they might feel like if they just get a job, lose weight, start exercising, or whatever the intangible might be, they might be able to start feeling better. If, if, if . . . but it is never that easy. Maybe they don't want to feel better. Maybe they feel so low that just getting through the day is often too much of an effort, so they stay in bed all day and block the world out. You don't know what they're feeling unless you are in their shoes.

This is where a support group would come in handy. Dealing with feelings of fear, sadness, anger, and resentment, and knowing that you're not alone in your feelings, might be just the help you need. Caretakers just do their best to help a depressed person cope. But you aren't a professional, so how much can you actually do for the person? Sure you can leave self-help books around, or pamphlets from organizations that help with depression, but you can't make someone read them. Just like you can't make someone call a hospital, psychiatrist, or counselor. He needs to seek the help himself, unless of course, it's gotten so bad that he must be hospitalized either willingly or against his will. If the person presents a danger to herself or those around her (in particular, you or your family members) or is unable to take care of her basic needs, then she might need psychiatric hospitalization. How do you know when it's come to that?

How to Know When Hospitalization Becomes Necessary

If a person has become a danger to himself, a danger to others, or unable to care for his own basic needs; risks financial ruin due to inability to function on a daily basis; or makes a suicide attempt(s), psychiatric hospitalization may be the only option left to consider. If the individual willingly goes to an emergency room, he will receive an assessment by a trained professional to see if his symptoms are severe enough that he needs to be hospitalized. If your loved one is *not* willing to go to the emergency room for an evaluation, then call 9-1-1 and law enforcement staff will help in getting that individual to the hospital for an assessment.

Each state has its own mental health laws. In most states, the person can sign herself in voluntarily if she meets the criteria for psychiatric hospitalization. But there are some patients who want to go to a hospital voluntarily and then have to wait months for a free bed. If she is unwilling to admit herself, clinically licensed professionals can involuntarily admit her. Due to each state having its own separate protocol, the staff at the emergency department will help facilitate the process, according to the laws of the state the hospital is in.

In the past, a person could just have a spouse held involuntarily by going to a magistrate and saying, for example, "My wife is crazy. You need to put her away." Because of that, a person could be held for extended lengths of time, even without receiving treatment, without any proof of diagnosis of mental illness. Now, according to Liza Gold, a forensic psychiatrist at the Georgetown University School of Medicine in Washington, DC, "The pendulum has swung 'too far,' because the law doesn't allow patients to be protected from themselves."[3]

In an online 2013 article, Liz Szabo offered a compelling argument about committing mentally ill adults. She quoted Ron Manderscheid, executive director of the National Association of County Behavioral Health and Developmental Disability Directors, who said, "If someone has cancer, they shouldn't have to wait until they have acute cancer and be dying in the next two weeks before we give them care. . . . But that's how we operate the mental health system."[4]

How Laws Vary by State—Involuntary Institutionalization

I picked three random states' laws to highlight. The three states are Arizona, Indiana, and Florida. Since each of the fifty states in the United States has its own laws regarding a person being involuntarily institutionalized if mentally ill, check out the grid to see how each state differs. These laws are to protect the person who is sick, as well as other people, from harm. To find out about your specific state, go to mentalillnesspolicy.org/studies/state-standards-involuntary-treatment.html, or find out how to initiate court-ordered assisted treatment in all fifty states' laws on the following website: www.treatmentadvocacycenter.org/legal-resources/state-standards/2265.

Table 8.1. Committing Someone with Mental Illness[1]

| Arizona Rev. Stat. § 36-531(B) § 36-520(A) § 36-524 | *For inpatient or outpatient commitment:* If it is determined upon an evaluation of the patient's condition that he [meets the state commitment standard], the medical director in charge of the agency which provided the evaluation shall . . . sign and file a petition for court-ordered treatment unless the county attorney performs the functions of preparing, signing or filing the petition as provided [elsewhere]. |

For emergency evaluation: Any responsible individual may apply for a court-ordered evaluation of a person who is alleged to be, as a result of a mental disorder, a danger to self or to others, persistently or acutely disabled, or gravely disabled [meet the state commitment standard] and who is unwilling or unable to undergo a voluntary evaluation.

A. A written application for emergency admission shall be made to an evaluation agency before a person may be hospitalized in the agency.

B. The application for emergency admission shall be made by a person with knowledge of the facts requiring emergency admission. The applicant may be a relative or friend of the person, a peace officer, the admitting officer or another responsible person.

Florida Stat.
§ 394.467(3)
§ 394.4655(3)
§ 394.463(2)(a)

For inpatient commitment: Petition for involuntary inpatient placement. The administrator of the facility shall file a petition for involuntary inpatient placement in the court in the county where the patient is located.

For outpatient commitment ("involuntary outpatient placement"): Petition for involuntary outpatient placement.

(a) A petition for involuntary outpatient placement may be filed by:

1. The administrator of a receiving facility; or 2. The administrator of a treatment facility.

For emergency evaluation ("involuntary examination"): An involuntary examination may be initiated by any one of the following means:

C. 1. A court may enter an ex parte order stating that a person appears to meet the criteria for involuntary examination, giving the findings on which that conclusion is based. The ex parte order for involuntary examination must be based on sworn testimony, written or oral.

D. 2. A law enforcement officer shall take a person who appears to meet the criteria for involuntary examination into custody and deliver the person or have him or her delivered to the nearest receiving facility for examination.

E. 3. A physician, clinical psychologist, psychiatric nurse, mental health counselor, marriage and family therapist, or clinical social worker may execute a certificate stating that he or she has examined a person within the preceding 48 hours and finds that the person appears to meet the criteria for involuntary examination and stating the observations upon which that conclusion is based.

Indiana Code Ann. § 12-26-7-2(b) § 12-26-6-2(b)	*For inpatient or outpatient commitment:* A proceeding for the commitment of an individual who appears to be suffering from a chronic mental illness may be begun by filing with a court having jurisdiction a written petition by any of the following:

(1) A health officer (2) A police officer (3) A friend of the individual (4) A relative of the individual (5) The spouse of the individual (6) A guardian of the individual (7) The superintendent of a facility where the individual is present (8) A prosecuting attorney in accordance with IC 35-36-2-4 (9) A prosecuting attorney or the attorney for a county office if civil commitment proceedings are initiated under IC 31-34-19-3 or IC 31-37-18-3 (10) A third party that contracts with the division of mental health and addiction to provide competency restoration services to a defendant under IC 35-36-3-3 or IC 35-36-3-4

For emergency evaluation: A petitioner under subsection (a)(3) must be at least eighteen (18) years of age.

[1]Treatment Advocacy Center, "Initiating Court-Ordered Assisted Treatment," www.treatment advocacycenter.org/legal-resources/state-standards/2265 (accessed March 6, 2014).

Feeling like the Parent and Not the Child

Has it become your task to care for your siblings? Perhaps you have your driver's license already and are now in charge of carpooling your siblings around to school and other various activities. Maybe it has become your task to make dinner or pack lunches for school. You may even be asked to give your little brother and sister a bath and put them to bed at night. "When did I become the head of the household?" you wonder. This isn't a fair position to be put in; however, it does happen frequently when a parent is disabled with such an affliction as a major depressive episode.

You might even have taken on the role of making your parent eat, when you are able to. Or you could be urging your father to wake up and shower, or imploring him to go to work. It should not be your task to motivate and care for an entire family, but somehow that's what's happened to you. What can you do to remedy the situation? How can you relinquish this role of caretaker? You need to confide in a trusted adult, one who can help. Perhaps you live in a single-parent household, or your other parent is in denial and just going about everyday life without acknowledging the added responsibilities you've taken on. You need to bring this situation out in the open. Talk to your parent who is not ill, or do research on the Internet to see what resources are available to you. (Many helpful resources are listed in the back of this book.) As a teen, your life is difficult enough to navigate, without being responsible for other human beings. Tell someone about your parent's depression. Perhaps you could even call your family doctor and ask his advice for how to get your parent the help she needs, especially if it is affecting the entire family.

Feeling Alone (Early Independence) with No Supervision or Caretaker

How can you get the care and attention you need? First of all, you might have to become more independent by keeping your life running smoothly on your own. When you get up, make your bed, shower and change clothes, brush your hair and teeth, and fix yourself something to eat. Pack a lunch, grab your homework, and head off to the bus for school. You might already have a part-time job. You'll have to figure out transportation on your own, whether it's riding the bus home, then walking to work, or calling a friend or coworker for a ride. For a while, you might have to figure things out on your own. This isn't an ideal situation, but for the time being, it is what it is. Do you have an adult in your life in whom you can confide? Perhaps an aunt, uncle, or cousin lives close by whom you can talk to and rely on for some help with your daily activities. Maybe there is a friend's parent or trusted neighbor who can help pick up the slack.

Feeling alone and isolated can trigger a depression in you. This is something you'd want to avoid. Your own mental health and well-being should not be at stake just because your parent is not functioning well. Do your best to practice positive self-talk such as, "Life is good and I can take care of my own world by myself for the moment," or "I studied hard for the test, and will do well at school today." Ways to keep yourself positive and continue making healthy choices are important steps to not allowing yourself to fall into a depression. There are support groups for families of depressed persons and caretakers. Remember: NAMI (www.nami.org) and DBSA (Depression and Bipolar Support Alliance; www.dbsalliance.org) are resources in place to help people in your situation. Use them to help yourself out!

Your Own Troubles at School

When you've allowed your own life to be altered by what's going on at home, this could be a warning sign to others that you, yourself, need help, too. Are your studies suffering, or are you truant to school, or skipping classes altogether? Perhaps you feel you can't help it, or you may even be doing it as a cry for help—for someone to notice what's going on at home and step in. This is a self-destructive action that will only hurt you in the end. Realize what you're doing, and try your best to end the pattern.

You might just be having trouble concentrating, worrying about your sick family member. Or you might be having trouble with a difficult class and just need a tutor to get you back on track. You can talk to a teacher to see if there is after-school help available for free. Maybe your teacher keeps office hours and can tutor you herself. Don't be afraid to ask for such help. You can't let your future plans drown because your family is having problems dealing with a loved one who is struggling with depression. Your life is important, and it's up to you to keep it on track.

Trouble with Relationships

Have you allowed your friendships to suffer or fall apart altogether? Maybe you've let a romantic relationship fall apart because your problems at home have become all consuming. This is not a healthy way to get through your life. You need the support of friends, boy- or girlfriends, and even friends' parents to keep you happy and healthy. Don't let these relationships fall by the wayside. These are the people who will help you feel safe, happy, and confident in all that you do each day. If you're ashamed to have friends over, then go hang out at their houses, or go play sports at a rec center, or visit the library to do homework together. You may be worried to leave a parent alone for long periods of time, but you just can't put your life on hold. It is unhealthy and unnatural. If your parent is truly struggling with the symptoms of severe depression, or is at risk of harming himself or others,

"I always keep an eye on [my father]. . . . I fly under that radar so he won't be combative; Dad would get vicious, and Mom shielded me. Then I shielded my two siblings (ages 17 and 14) from verbal and physical abuse. I'd get away when possible."—William, age 19[d]

"Rx helps [my father] but he won't take it. The rare times that he does, he's a doll . . . a real teddy bear. Plus, nutrition is a factor. If he doesn't eat and gets low blood sugar, it will really make symptoms flare up. He only buys food on the days before visitation with us kids. Dad doesn't exercise. There's plenty he could do but he refuses. It's like my dad has a fear of acceptance of the illness [bipolar]. His relationship with his grandparents [he was adopted] was complex. They did not accept him as 'family.'"—William, age 19[e]

then he should be taken to the emergency department of your local hospital and evaluated by a professional to see if he needs to be admitted. Hospitalization may be a necessary consideration, and you should talk to your guidance counselor about intervening. Do not try to handle everything on your own.

Avoidance of Parent

Maybe you've decided to avoid your parent altogether. Do you stay away from your father at all costs? Sometimes you barely see him at all, and when you do, you answer with sharp yes or no answers to questions. This isn't going to help you or him. While it might help you to avoid seeing a parent's decline in health, it will only add to your worry and feelings of guilt if something bad were to happen to him.

Try your best to get your parent to seek help. Maybe you're avoiding your mother as a "tough love" tactic, saying something like, "If you're not going to get help, then I'm just not going to associate with you." How has that worked for you so far? Not so well, I'd imagine. I can't stress enough how you need to get another adult involved with finding solutions. Is your other parent living with the family? Perhaps you can confide in her. Tell her something like, "Dad's depression is taking a toll on my life, and making it hard for me to function. I need help!" Your healthy parent might be focusing on your sick parent way too much, and not taking the time to notice what effect it is having on you. You need to speak up and make your needs known. The disorder of depression affects the entire family as a unit, so don't try to handle everything on your own all of the time.

HOW VARIOUS SUBGROUPS DEAL WITH DEPRESSION

Members of various subgroups can develop depression due to the stress of being part of a certain community. Some examples are the military; various religious faiths; gay, lesbian, bisexual, and transgendered (GLBT) individuals; diverse ethnicities; diverse cultures; and the disabled—just to name a few.

If you feel very different from your friends, neighbors, peers, or other members of your subgroup, you might have various risk factors for being susceptible to depression. This chapter is just a brief overview of some of the various groups who deal with depression.

Military Families: Sacrifices Made for Us All

American soldiers have a challenging task in protecting our country. There is a level of stress that military men and women experience on a daily basis, which sometimes includes dealing with multiple deployments overseas for long periods of time. In this chapter, there is a focus on another subgroup of people that sometimes get forgotten: the *families* of the military personnel who are prone to depression. These families are made up of spouses, children, and teens, as well as parents, siblings, and grandparents of those who serve and protect our country. It takes family, along with friends and community, to support soldiers with what they go through to do their jobs every day.

If you are a teen or young adult in the military, you know firsthand the pressures and stress put on you, the soldier. You have risk factors for major depressive disorder, among other types of depression, along with post-traumatic stress disorder. It is imperative that you reach out to receive the medical treatment you need and deserve!

Military branches.

Difficulties Saying Goodbye and Hello and Goodbye Again

Sean O'Leary is fourteen years old but still feels the impact of 9/11, which happened when he was a toddler. Both of his parents serve in the U.S. Army Reserve. In 2013, his dad, Major Pat O'Leary, was away on his second deployment in five years. Sean said his peers don't have a clue about what he's going through.

"I used to tell kids that my parents are in the military, and they would just say, 'Oh cool! Have they ever killed anybody?'" Sean said. "That really bothered me that that was the first question they asked me—and they thought it was really cool."[1]

! Children in Military Families Experiencing Depression

According to the National Alliance on Mental Illness in its family booklet, "Children in military families also experience higher rates of depression than the general population with one in four of them experiencing symptoms of depression."[a]

With America at war for more than a decade, many reservists like Major O'Leary have been deployed multiple times. More than 628,000 kids have had to say good-bye to their parents, and the impact on these children has not been extensively researched yet. What has been observed by Janine Boldrin is that "younger children have trouble sleeping, while older children get into more trouble, and have attachment issues with the returning parent," according to her article "How Are the Kids?" in the *Officer* magazine.[2]

In the same article, a nonprofit agency called Our Military Kids (www.our militarykids.org) is mentioned. The organization provides activity grants for the children of deployed members of the Reserve Component and wounded and fallen warriors from all military components. Our Military Kids completed a survey on children in military families, and found that "nearly sixty percent of parents reported attention difficulties with their kids. Nearly half reported emotional reactivity/mood swings, and more than one-third reported anxiety/depression." The article went on to say, "Studies on deployment-impacted military children reported that one in five children coped poorly or very poorly due to deployment separation. Depression and school problems were reported in one in five children. High levels of sadness were found in all age groups."[3]

One problem often repeated in the article was that families who do not live on a military post, but rather in an average community, do not get the support they need. Neighbors and friends in the community don't know what the family is going through and cannot really empathize.

Stress of Moving Continuously

Have you ever had to move to a new home? Was it in the same town, or even to a new state? I'll bet that was an experience that changed your life. Having to say good-bye to your friends and your home, and make all new friends and be "the new kid" can be difficult for many people. Now imagine having to do that over and over again every couple of years. Wow! Can you even imagine that? After moving a few times, you may begin to streamline your belongings, not hanging on to things as much as you used to. Perhaps your prized possessions are your photos and memories. Does this sound familiar to you? Then you might be in an active duty military family.

Fitting in at New Schools

Who likes to be the new kid at school? Okay, maybe sometimes you fantasize what it would be like to be able to reinvent yourself and not have the same kids you've gone to school with "forever" know every little thing about you. But, truly, isn't there a comfort in having the same friends for a really long time?

What if you had to change schools every year or two, sometimes more often than that? Seriously, close your eyes and imagine what that must feel like. You might want to put up barriers and not get too close to people since you'll have to leave them soon anyway, right? (Not the best idea, but it does happen.) I asked teens of military personnel the best way they found to be the new kid in their new schools. Seventeen-year-old Erin responded, "At first, it was a little difficult to always be the new kid in school, basically restarting your life every three years. But after a while, you become used to it and view it as more of a new adventure. Making new friends and being accepted was the most stressful part of moving a lot." Erin's family has moved seven times in her lifetime![4]

Finding Out Your Parent Is Being Deployed

With her father in the military her whole life, Erin (a junior in high school at the time of this interview) has never known life any other way. She said that her dad has been deployed off and on for sixteen of her seventeen years of life. When asked about her feelings after her father's return in 2013 she said, "I was indifferent. It was a little surreal because it was weird to think my dad was finally coming home. It's hard to grasp that after so much time spent apart he was finally coming

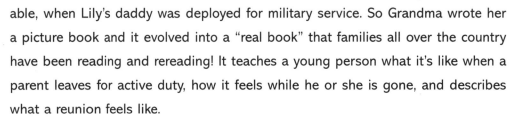

Exceptional Children's Book: Lily Hates Goodbyes

Author Jerilyn Marler tried to soothe her granddaughter Lily, who was nearly inconsolable, when Lily's daddy was deployed for military service. So Grandma wrote her a picture book and it evolved into a "real book" that families all over the country have been reading and rereading! It teaches a young person what it's like when a parent leaves for active duty, how it feels while he or she is gone, and describes what a reunion feels like.

You can get *Lily Hates Goodbyes* at www.amazon.com/Jerilyn-Marler/e/B001K8TC1Y/ or go to your local library; you can even view a portion of the book, set to music, on YouTube.com. Share this with your little brother, or sister, or someone you love. You'll be glad you did![b]

Erin's Story: What It's Like When a Parent Is Gone for Many Months (Active Duty)

"My dad would send us lots of letters and call my mother every night. When he was deployed my whole family tried to keep each other really busy with sports and clubs and things. This helped make the time go by faster. My dad also worked out a lot when he was deployed, he told me," said Erin, a seventeen-year-old high school junior.

When asked how she copes with the separation of her dad from her family, Erin replied, "I run a lot. I'm on varsity track and cross-country [teams]. Running allows me to ease my mind and go off in my own world that's anxiety free. I also just try to relax, hang out with friends and family, and just keep busy."[c]

---

home. I was so happy, but at the same time, I was almost in disbelief because it felt like it hadn't really been a year."[5]

It wasn't always that way though. When asked to think back on earlier times when her father returned from deployment, Erin shared this story:

I remember when I was in first grade, my dad was returning from Iraq for the first time and it was to be a surprise. But I had an inkling that he was coming home and for some strange reason I woke up in the middle of the night. It was like I knew he was coming home even though my parents didn't tell me. And sure enough he came home that morning![6]

Lesbian, Gay, Bisexual, and Transgendered American Teens

LGBT Teens

In American culture, there are various prejudices against gay and transgendered people. Great strides have been made for same-sex marriages in the past couple of years; however, there continues to be some discrimination. When a lesbian, gay, or bisexual person publicly "comes out," people are often not supportive.

In 1997, comedian and celebrity Ellen DeGeneres was on the cover of *Time* magazine with the caption, "Yep, I'm Gay!" This was a huge inspiration for young gay Americans, in particular, to have the courage and strength to come

Lesbian teens.

out to friends and family. But her declaration didn't come without a price. Her sitcom at the time was cancelled, followed by another unsuccessful TV show. Not everyone was supportive.

Flash forward to 2014, and Ellen has had a successful daytime talk show since September 2003; has been married to her partner, Portia de Rossi, since 2008; has won awards; and has hosted awards shows. But the road she chose was not always smooth, although she is credited with becoming the first openly gay sitcom star.

What does being gay have to do with depression? Many external triggers are present when a person decides to come out. Hate crimes and prejudice are two of them that can cause a person to have depressive episodes. Being shunned by family, coworkers, friends, or their religion is another way that gay people are treated unfairly, which can lead to depression.

Sexuality: Do Differences Such as Homosexuality Increase Risk of Depression in American Culture?

The teen years are notorious for low self-esteem, lack of self-confidence, and introspection. Feeling apart from others can play a large role in depression. If a teen is gay, not only does he or she have to deal with being "different" from the majority of his or her friends, but there is prejudice, stereotyping, insults, confusion from others, and even abuse. With bullying, hazing, and other such abusive behaviors rampant in American high schools and in communities today, it is not only brave to come out as a gay person, but dangerous sometimes, as well. Many schools say publicly that they have adopted a zero-tolerance policy for bullying, hazing, and hate crimes, but it's still hard to legally prosecute offenders

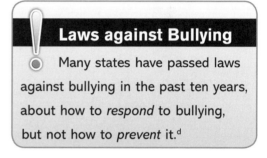

Laws against Bullying

Many states have passed laws against bullying in the past ten years, about how to *respond* to bullying, but not how to *prevent* it.[d]

who are minors and in school. As of 2013, there are no federal antibullying laws in place. President Obama has supported and endorsed the Student Nondiscrimination Act, which was written to protect teens from harassment due to their gender or sexuality, but it has not yet become law.[7]

The Numbers—Comparing Depression in Gay Teens and Heterosexual Teens

According to a 2001 study by Susan Cochran, PhD, various population-based public health studies found that in lesbian and gay youth, there are higher rates of major depression, generalized anxiety disorder, and substance use or dependence. The study went on to report higher rates of anxiety, mood and substance use disorders, and suicidal thoughts among people ages fifteen to fifty-four with same-sex partners. Lastly, there seemed to be a higher reported use of mental health services in men and women reporting same-sex partners.[8]

However, in her 2002 study, Tori DeAngelis states that gay and lesbian youth are only slightly more likely than heterosexual youth to attempt suicide, compared to what was originally thought in the past.[9]

Deb's Story: Coming Out in Her Early 20s

Deb is a gay adult who came out when she was 23. She waited past her teen years to acknowledge her sexual orientation. "I came out when I was 23, when I knew I was confident enough to handle any reaction from friends and family, good or bad. I was very fortunate that almost all people I knew were supportive. . . . [My parents] have been supportive ever since. I'm truly lucky."

When Deb was asked if she ever suffered from depression, she replied,

Yes, I think I have that low-grade constant depression [dysthemia], and probably have had it most of my life. I don't think it's hormonal or from puberty. It's something I have struggled with my whole life. I don't take meds for it though shrinks have suggested I do. I gave up drinking and smoking because neither is good for depression. I try to exercise and stay healthy because that affects it. [As a teen,] playing sports probably saved my life. I played volleyball, basketball, and softball until I left for college; and my favorite thing was riding the bus with my teams to away games. We'd play music and sing.[e]

In a study by Caitlin Ryan, PhD, it was suggested that GLBT adults who reported high rates of parental rejection in their teens were 8.4 times more likely to report having attempted suicide, 5.9 times more likely to report high levels of depression, 3.4 times more likely to use illegal drugs, and 3.4 times more likely to have had unprotected sex than peers who reported no or low levels of family rejection.[10]

Since family acceptance is so important in the teen years, any rejection or implied rejection to a teen can feel catastrophic. This is proven in the numbers of suicide attempts, along with depression and "risky behaviors."

Native Americans

The percentage of Native American people in the United States with mental illness is at epidemic proportion compared to the rest of the population.

According to Brandy Judson, director of a suicide prevention program, during an NPR (National Public Radio) broadcast on September 12, 2013, the Native American population has a suicide rate that is four times higher than the national

When a Parent Is Homosexual Do the Kids Have Higher Depression Rates?

With many homosexual couples opting to have children, there is a generation of kids being raised in gay and lesbian households. This is much more common today than in generations of the past. Does depression have an impact on these children?

When using the search engine Google on the Internet, I posed the question of whether depression rates increase in same-sex households. After reading study after study found through that search, I concluded that the only reason kids in homosexual households would be more prone to depression than children in a heterosexual household is due to prejudices of other people, *not* from the fact that one or both of the parents are gay. It is the social pressures to conform to an old school stereotypical "nuclear family" that makes kids of the "2K generation" feel different than the majority of society.

average. This community is afflicted with mental illness such as depression and anxiety, not to mention the problem of substance abuse, the most prevalent of which is alcoholism. Budget cuts have affected this group in the past, and in 2013 there was a 5 percent budget cut in funding for mental health services, including suicide prevention.[11]

Judson runs the suicide prevention program at Native Americans for Community Action, a free or low-cost mental and physical health care facility in Flagstaff, Arizona. In the same 2013 NPR broadcast, Judson stated that the suicide prevention program has been very effective when it's fully funded. She helped identify several young people in a school who had prior attempts or extreme thoughts of suicide. When she was able to reconnect and follow up with the students a year later, she found that through counseling they were feeling better and had fewer suicidal thoughts. The problem is that 80 percent of her organization's budget comes from the federal government, which sustains the program. With cuts, it makes it nearly impossible. Judson said that the depression and suicide rate are long-term problems that will take decades to fix, and that it's not just a three-year job.[12]

Statistics on American Indian and Alaska Native Communities' Mental Health

- Approximately 26 percent of American Indians and Alaska Natives (AI/AN) live in poverty compared to 13 percent of the general population and 10 percent of Caucasian Americans.
- According to the Northern Plains study, 61 percent of the children had experienced a traumatic event.
- High prevalence of substance abuse and alcohol dependence is tied to a high risk for concurrent mental health problems.
- The prevalence of suicide is a strong indication of the necessity of mental health services in the AI/AN community. Suicide rates are particularly high among Native American males ages fifteen to twenty-four, who account for 64 percent of all suicides by AI/AN individuals.
- Available evidence suggests that mental illnesses (such as depression) impact approximately 20 percent of the total AI/AN population.[f]

Suicide Rates among Ethnicities

According to the National Institute of Mental Health's website, American Indians and Alaska Natives tend to have the highest rate of suicides, followed by non-Hispanic whites. Hispanics tend to have the lowest rate of suicides, while African Americans tend to have the second lowest rate.[g]

Various Religious Groups

If you look at a survey of various religious groups within the United States, it breaks down in the following fashion, according to Pew Research's Religion and Public Life Project:

- Christian—78.4 percent (includes Catholic, Mormon, Jehovah's Witness, Orthodox, and "other")
- Unaffiliated—16.1 percent (atheist, agnostic, and "nothing in particular")
- Jewish—1.7 percent

- Buddhist—0.7 percent
- Muslim—0.6 percent
- Hindu—0.4 percent
- Other world religions—less than 0.3 percent[13]

This breakdown shows how it might be easy for some teens to feel "different" than their peers for their religious beliefs. Growing up in a largely Jewish community in the suburbs of Chicago, I had no idea that there was such a small percentage of Jewish Americans in the United States. I thought, naïvely, that maybe 70 percent of Americans were Jewish. It shocked me to find out the percentage is quite small.

Arab American teen.

When researching religion and depression in teens, I found opposing views regarding the relationship between religions, faith, and depression. Are depressed people more apt to turn toward religion to make themselves feel better? Or are religious people who are firm in their beliefs less apt to have depression because they feel there is a higher power that loves them unconditionally? This debate has opinions for both sides, along with a view that religious affiliation has no impact on depression at all.

Arab Americans

Following 9/11 and the "war on terrorism," Arab Americans have faced more scrutiny than in the past. With racial profiling at places like airports, bus stations, and even on the streets, Arab American teens can feel self-conscious and unwelcomed in their own country.

The American Arab Forum website (for Arab and Muslim American Affairs) had this to say on the subject of Arab American teens and depression: "In a study commissioned by the Sesame Workshop, Arab-American children were found to be suffering from "vivid and immediate" anxieties and a "sense of shame" about violence in the United States.[14] According to a study at Wayne State University, 43 percent of a group of Arab-American teens were found to be depressed.[15]

On the Arab American Forum website, an article by Engy Abdelkader also reported the following: "Arab-American youth are not alone. Children perceived to be Middle Eastern, South Asian and/or Muslim are also targeted indiscriminately. According to a 2012 civil rights report published by the Council on American Islamic Relations, there was a thirty-one percent increase in reported cases of discrimination in school against kids perceived to be Muslim."[16]

When people are persecuted, they might fall prey to depressive episodes. No one likes to feel different or disliked, so one suggestion to battle these feelings may be to join a group that celebrates your differences. What are some cultural differences you can celebrate as an Arab teen? Are there holidays, particular cultural foods or clothing, or religious practices that make you feel special? Can you share some of these differences with your non-Arab friends? Although you might find the differences easier to see outwardly, there are more similarities between you and your peers than differences.

If you begin to feel self-conscious, just take a look at those around you. You may like the same books, movies, TV shows, music, and other pop culture things. Your favorite pastimes are probably similar as well. Perhaps you are a dancer, an athlete, a singer, a poet, or a big reader. Celebrate what makes you similar to others.

Special Needs Populations

Physically Challenged Teens

When you see someone who is physically challenged, do you treat him or her differently? Do you find yourself wondering what you would do if faced with such challenges? This is a common feeling when noticing someone who is different from you. But imagining yourself in their shoes isn't always enough help to those in need. Do any of your friends have physical challenges?

There was a discussion on About.com regarding whether it's more difficult for someone who recently became physically challenged or someone who has faced certain challenges from birth. A teen may have had a disability resulting from her delivery, or a genetic problem that caused the disability. I'm not entirely sure it matters which situation is more difficult, the point is that if you are a teen facing physical challenges, whether newly faced or present from birth, you may have feelings of depression. While you may be receiving treatments or therapies to handle your physical challenges, consider making sure your emotional needs are met, as well.

Do you have a caregiver who helps you throughout the day? Is this someone you are particularly close to and confide in? If not, you could ask another adult or even your family doctor questions about any depressed feelings you may be experiencing. Sure, as a teen you might feel sad or down for a few days, but when it lasts longer than two or more weeks and you're feeling hopeless or helpless, then it's time to talk to someone. Your doctor may address your physical needs, but does that physician take the time to ask about your emotional well-being? Be brave and bring it up if you are struggling.

If you're still in school, perhaps you could schedule a private meeting with your guidance counselor. He or she might have references for support groups that you might find helpful. The counselor may have literature, too, on teen depression, or even more specifically information about other teens that face similar challenges to what you are facing. The most important thing you can do for yourself is to reach out. Don't be too proud to ask for help!

Learning Disabled Teens

Have you heard your parent or teacher label you with some fancy term like *ADD* or *autistic* or some other name that makes you feel different? This can be difficult for anyone to handle, especially a teen. You don't necessarily want to be different than everyone else! Like most people, you just want to fit in. Has this certain label made you self-conscious or even shy? In one of the worst-case scenarios, it may even lead to some depressive feelings. Again, I'm not talking about everyday sadness that we all experience for a day or two at a time. I mean a depressive episode that lasts for a while, weeks even, without any foreseeable ending in sight.

You may feel different from your peers, but as mentioned before, there often are more similarities than differences between people. How do you handle your personal struggles? Do you reach out for help, confide in a friend, family member, or adult? Hopefully, you do not turn to unhealthy coping mechanisms such as substance abuse or self-harm to cope with your feelings. Many times people such as parents or caregivers are so caught up in helping you with your academic struggles that they don't realize your learning disability is taking a toll on your emotions as well. This is your chance, as a teen, to take a step toward adulthood and reach out for help. Be honest. Tell someone how you are feeling and ask for support in helping you feel better. Perhaps talk therapy or counseling might help you navigate your feelings and give you techniques to help cope. The worst thing you can do is nothing at all. This will only add to your feelings of aloneness in your struggles.

There are often local support groups for teens who are faced with the same challenges as you. For example, if you've been diagnosed with attention deficit disorder (ADD) or attention-deficit/hyperactivity disorder (ADHD), check out the following site on the Internet: www.mdjunction.com. Type "Teen ADD" or "ADHD in Teens" in the search bar and you'll see a bunch of choices come up. The same is true for other struggles, labels, or disorders teens (and adult caregivers) are faced with. The MDJunction website's tagline states "Online Support Groups for your Health Challenges: MDJunction is an active center for online support groups, a place where thousands meet every day to discuss their feelings, questions and hopes with like minded friends." This is just one of many possible support options you can find with a search engine such as Google or Bing on the World Wide Web.

To reiterate how various subgroups deal with depression, it is the same for other groups. Human beings just want to feel accepted and that they belong. Depression is a condition that can be managed, if you acknowledge it and reach out for help. Don't be afraid to stand out from the crowd if you need to. It can make a world of difference!

FINDING HELP FOR DEPRESSION SUFFERERS AND THE CAREGIVERS WHO LOVE THEM

Parents/Adult Relatives

In an ideal world, a parent, grandparent, aunt, or uncle is present in your life and offers you love, support, and guidance. Some adult relative is there for you to emulate, and hopefully confide in, when necessary. It's often hard to bare your soul to people who are not your age, for you may fear they won't understand you or where you are coming from. But they were your age once, too, even if it doesn't seem like it.

Granted, "times are different now" is a feeling most teens and adults share. It's important to bridge the gap between generations since there are some similar experiences that will be constant throughout the ages. First loves, first heart-breaks, first lessons such as driving or taking exams, first jobs, first college applications, and first rejections are milestones that older and younger generations may experience. Believe it or not, your mom or dad had her or his heart broken once or twice before! You are not alone, no matter how alone you might be feeling right now.

A parent is one of the first options to go to for help . . . assuming the relationship you have is generally a good one. If your family situation isn't one you can trust to help you get through your depressive episodes, then there are other avenues. But for now, let's discuss situations where family members *are* there for you.

"As far as my dad is concerned, it feels a lot like babysitting him from time to time. It's like walking on a tightrope, as you don't know when he'll be in a good mood or a bad mood. There's also this compulsion to apologize on his behalf. It's ultimately quite exhausting. [He is bipolar.]

"It's frustrating because it ultimately comes down to helping himself. If he isn't willing to get help, there's little I can do. Thus, I must focus my efforts on containing his behavior, having it affect as few people as possible."

—William, age 19[a]

Have you tried to approach the adults in your life to tell them when you're feeling down? It's important to have trust. Trust that they will be able to help you reach out to the necessary people who can help you. A parent, for example, might be able to help you find resources such as the National Alliance on Mental Illness (NAMI; www.nami.org). There are over 1,000 affiliates around the United States to help you with a variety of special needs such as depression, bipolar disorder, and anxiety, just to name a few. NAMI has local teen support groups where you can talk to other teens that face similar issues you may be dealing with. Go to the website to find a chapter near you.

It's important for your parents, aunts, uncles, and/or grandparents to seek help for themselves as well. It can be physically exhausting to care for you in the low times. Some places they can seek help are NAMI (www.nami.org), Psych-Central (psychcentral.com/lib/2010/self-care-for-depression-caregivers/), and MDJunction (www.mdjunction.com).

Parents Help by Setting Limits and Boundaries

When you, as a teen or young adult, isolate, it is a major warning sign for parents and those who love you. Sure many teens spend a lot of time alone in their rooms, but when it becomes truly noticeable, sometimes a parent must intervene. She might try to get you out and about around family members. Something as seemingly simple as making everyone sit at the dinner table together each night could prove to be helpful.

Another way a parent might reach out to you is by setting rules and enforcing them. Curfew is a big one. If you are expected home at a certain time and do not comply, it might mean taking away certain privileges such as the car or use of cell

Confiding in your parents.

phone. Boundaries are set for your protection and to show that your parent cares for you and your well-being, not to mention that there may be laws in your town that restrict teens hours out at night as well. If you don't comply with your town's curfew, your decision could impact your parents legally, as well.

Siblings

Not everyone can say he or she has the best relationship with a sibling. My advice to my own children is that they always have to make up after any fight with their

"When I was around twelve years old, I took off for several hours on my bike. I had nowhere to go, and didn't feel there was anyone I could talk to. I was so upset, but not about anything in particular. I know now, that I was depressed. I had begun to isolate myself, and not want to be around anyone I knew or cared about, not friends or family. After wandering around my town for several hours, my mom finally found me and took me home. Although I never told her, I was secretly glad that she cared enough to search for me."—CGS, 20-something[b]

siblings because friends will come and go, as will boyfriends and girlfriends, but siblings are the one relationship you will have for your entire life. You will know them even longer than you know your parents, most likely.

But life isn't always fair, and people don't always have a loving relationship with members of their family just because they are blood relatives. In fact, many families are highly dysfunctional. If you find yourself in this situation, do what's best for you mentally, and find another person, someone besides a sibling, to confide in.

Let's assume, for the sake of this example, that you *do* have a good relationship with at least one of your siblings. Try to approach the subject of your feelings (such as depression) with her. You may be surprised to find she has similar feelings. Between dealing with the same family issues that you are and sharing similar genetics (depression can be hereditary), a sibling might have depression, too, but was afraid to discuss it with *you*. So it might be a good idea to "test the waters" and confide in a brother or sister to see if either has ever felt depressed, and what each has done to help deal with such feelings. If a sibling does not suffer from depression, perhaps he can be a sounding board for you to get your feelings out, and to talk through your down periods. It helps to have someone you love and trust listen to you when you need to vent your feelings.

Being a confidante can be draining for sisters or brothers, and they need to reach out for help, as well. Whether they seek counseling, or help themselves with a support group, it is important that they have somewhere to turn to process their feelings about your depression. Perhaps you have turned to unhealthy coping mechanisms, many of which could weigh heavily on siblings. They might feel partly responsible if you harm yourself. Siblings can feel helpless when your depression spirals downward, and they are unable to help. Share the information with your brothers and sisters that they, too, need help. Tell them about NAMI, PsychCentral, and MDJunction. Perhaps you could even invite them to attend a support group meeting with you. You could also check out your local community center to see if they offer any youth services. Don't discount your local religious community, either, if you are of a certain faith. Many religious organizations have teen groups, or youth groups, in order to promote peer interaction.

Friends

This is more tricky. Friends are people you see the most and talk to the most on a day-to-day basis. They know about your life at school or maybe work with you at a part-time job and know your social circle. But who can you truly trust with your most intimate secrets? Many people who suffer from depression keep it a secret by *pretending* everything is fine. Are you one of these people? As a teen, I was very smiley and nice to everyone. If I was without a smile people would say, "Oh my God! What's wrong? If *you're* not happy, something must be totally wrong with the world." That was a lot of pressure to live up to. I was always the goofy one to joke around and make everyone laugh. I couldn't have an *off* day. Anytime I even seemed a tiny bit down or depressed, I would be talked about, so I always just smiled and laughed things off in public, and often cried in private. I never told my friends about my depression, or my siblings either, for that matter. I share this with readers as a caution—*please* don't make this mistake. Find *someone* to share your feelings with. You can seek help in your teens and not waste many, many years suffering alone like I did! If you do confide in your friends, maybe you could go to a support group together.

Your Response to Someone Else's Depression

Whether you believe it or not, your reaction to your friend or loved one's depressed mood can add to the outcome. If you're frustrated with him, he'll know it. This is pressure that he doesn't need. Do your best not to be judgmental about whatever mood he might be feeling.

What to Do If a Friend Confesses Suicidal Thoughts, Thoughts of Harming Others, or Risky Behavior

You might be afraid of risking a friendship if you tell someone else about a friend's confession of suicidal thoughts. Nothing could be further from the truth. You may be saving that person's life! The first thing you can do is listen to your friend talk. Let him get his feelings off his chest. He may need you to be a sounding board for his suicidal thoughts. Remember not to minimize what he is

> ## Kevin's Story: "Confessions of a Depressed Comic"
>
> Kevin Breel was a popular student athlete, honor roll student, stand-up comedian, and teenager. When he confessed to the world that he lives with depression, Kevin found everyone to be surprised. He talks about the epidemic proportions of depression and how not enough is being done about it. Kevin began his talk saying there are two selves people represent, the first being what people outwardly think of you and the second being your true self that you don't let many people see. "Not my problem" is the attitude in America that he hopes to change. Kevin's speech is touching and has lots of great information from a teen who seems to have it all, yet struggles daily with major depression. Check it out by going to www.youtube.com/watch?v=VYs05qPycYQ.

telling you by saying something you hope is helpful such as, "It'll be okay, you're just having a bad day." To your friend, thoughts of death may be all consuming. It might be what he thinks about every waking moment. Although suicide is often an impulse action, many times it is thought about for quite a while before something triggers that person to finally take action. It is important that you take him and his threat very seriously. (See statistics in chapter 5, "Unhealthy Coping Mechanisms.")

The same can be said if a friend brags that he is going to harm others. Many of the school shootings in America had warnings such as the offenders talking about what they were going to do, but people didn't report it in time. If your friend talks about doing harm to others, you *need* to tell an authority!

As a young person yourself, you are not equipped to handle your friend's depression. That is why it is imperative for you to seek the help of a professional adult. I repeat, it is imperative to seek help! You may feel guilty for "ratting out your friend," but it is a dangerous situation he is discussing with you. If you are to tell someone about your discussion, what is the worst thing that could happen—your friend never speaks to you again? Think of the alternative, if you *don't* tell someone else who can help. That friend, or even others, could die! So although it seems like a tough decision to make, it truly is a no brainer. Go to someone you know and trust, such as a teacher, a coach, a guidance counselor, a parent, a priest or rabbi—someone. There are anonymous hotlines you can call as well, and phone numbers are listed in other chapters of this book. Remember, validate your friend's feelings and beg her to seek help. Offer to go with her to a support

A Great Read: Wintergirls

Wintergirls is a book by Laurie Halse Anderson in which two girls struggle with eating disorders and depression. They are best friends. One reaches out to the other for support—too late. Their dangerous game of who can be the thinnest comes to an abrupt end when one girl dies, while the survivor tries to hold out hope that she can recover before it's too late for her, as well.[c]

group, or to find a trusted adult who can help her with these feelings. Maybe she needs counseling; maybe she will even need the medical attention of a psychiatrist to get medication or other therapies. But if your friend thinks about ending his life, he definitely needs some kind of medical intervention! Being a teen yourself, you are not a professional, so don't be too hard on yourself if you don't know the exact right thing to do or say. Being a friend and telling the person that you love her and are here to help in any way possible is a great place to start.

Teachers/Mentors

If you find it too difficult to let your friends or family in on your depression, or if you just want to keep your private life private, it can help to find an objective adult. Do you have a particular teacher that you feel you could confide in? Perhaps there is a mentor such as a music teacher, or the head of a club you are in. This person could be more objective than the people who are closest to you. A teacher who knows you in one particular setting, such as photography club, might know of some of your talents that others do not know about. Perhaps you have a good one-on-one relationship with that person. This is an adult who might be ideal to confide in when you're having a low period. He might just be someone who can listen, which is so helpful!

Even if a person in whom you confided doesn't have any answers for you, or any suggestions about what to do about your feelings or a particular situation, it's nice to have someone that cares and can listen while you let out your sadness. But remember to be thankful to him or her, and not angry if he or she doesn't know the exact right thing to say to make you feel better. That person is doing his best, too, to help you get through a tough time.

"I think trying to reach out to religious leaders, IF you know them very well already, can be helpful. I went to my math teacher. I found it easier to go to a woman. She seemed to have maternal instincts. My male teacher was a new parent, and over six feet tall. My talks with teachers at lunchtime helped tremendously. I had an epiphany that I couldn't keep it a secret—my Dad's illness—it was making me physically ill. It helped to talk to someone not in the family unit. But I also didn't want DCFS [Department of Children and Family Services] called."—William, age 19[d]

Coaches/Activity Leaders

No one understands the pressure you're under more than a coach, your band director, or the director of a play you might be in. They may understand the demands that are placed on you, and might listen with an empathetic ear. They could be able to offer suggestions that helped them deal with the pressures of being an athlete or performer when they were younger.

Most athletes feel a certain comfort level with their coaches, and hopefully this is something you feel, too, if you're involved with sports. A coach is someone who spends a lot of time with you, often several hours a day. If you are clinically depressed, you may have quit the team or dropped out of a play or given up other things that used to make you happy. Hopefully, you are reading this before your depression sinks that low, but in either case, whether you're still on the team or not, reach out to people who really know you, such as coaches. They will probably have noticed a change in your mood or personality if your depression has become really bad. They might feel gratitude or relief that you're brave enough to come forward to share your feelings.

Codependency

If there are people you have been talking to about your feelings of depression, they might need help as well. It is difficult to watch someone with depression suffer; this person might even develop something called *codependency*. What this means is that your caregiver or confidant, for example, ties in his or her feelings to how *you* are doing mentally. If you are suffering, he takes too much of that on his own shoulders. He feels a responsibility for your feelings, or suffers if he is unable to help you out. On the same note, if you have codependent tendencies, that

> ## Self-Help Groups for a Variety of Problems That Could Trigger Depressive Feelings
>
> Alcoholics Anonymous (AA)
>
> Co-Dependents Anonymous (CODA)
>
> For Families of Alcoholics (Al-Anon)
>
> Gamblers Anonymous (GA)
>
> National Alliance on Mental Illness (NAMI)
>
> Overeaters Anonymous (OA)

means you let someone else's mood guide yours. If your boyfriend, for example, is very angry or even sad, you let that set the tone for your mood, and you may then feel edgy or sad, too.

There is an organization called Co-Dependents Anonymous, and it has a website, www.coda.org. You can log on to find out about meetings near you if you feel you are codependent or want to learn more about what that truly means. There is also a book titled *Codependent No More*, by Melody Beattie, which you might find helpful.[1] (The author has written several books on the topic.)

How the Family Can Function as a Unit without the Depression Always Being the Center of Attention

Although your depression might make you feel so low that you cannot get out of bed, or shower, or come to the dinner table, do your best to muster up all of your strength to participate with the family. Perhaps you can agree to a family counseling session to consider everyone else's feelings.

It is tough to hear, but everything cannot always be about you and your depression. You've got to do whatever it takes to take a step toward a healthier you. It may be as involved as agreeing to try a combination of medication and therapy. Sometimes, you have to put aside your pride and just *try* to get better, even if it means admitting you need help!

Be an active participant in your family dynamic. What did you do as a child for fun—play board games with your family, cards, or sports? Why not do those things again? Perhaps you had a hobby you enjoyed such as scrapbooking or photography. Although it may seem like a tall order, if you are engaged with the family unit, this might help pull you out of the darkness you are feeling. Use your family as a tool for strength and encouragement.

If you are a caretaker or loved one of someone who is depressed, use the ideas mentioned to help engage people. Doing things together is a great way to help lift someone's spirits, letting the person know you care about her, even when she may not feel particularly lovable.

Dealing with a Depressed Person's Limitations

Who is the depressed person in your life? Is it a brother or sister, a cousin, a friend from school or your neighborhood? He may have limitations on what he can do in a day. On bad days, it might be a huge stretch for him to just get out of bed, eat, maybe brush his teeth, and actually be seen by family members in his own house. Risking an interaction with other people is a huge hurdle for someone who is in a deep depression. She may not want to have to interact with anyone in the outside world. That is why it is so difficult to actually get out of bed when depressed. Wanting to simply pull the covers over her head and block out the whole world and avoid acknowledging any part of her life may be what all the sleeping is about. This is very limiting for her and could be a huge frustration to you!

Perhaps you've made plans several times with a friend, and she always ends up cancelling or just not showing up at all without a call or text to cancel. This is an important time for you to empathize with her and try to see the world through her eyes. She isn't doing it to piss you off or be a bad friend. She is simply self-preserving herself and doing whatever she needs to in order to make it through the day. While it may be testing your patience as a friend or loved one, remember the good parts in your relationship and don't give up on her. This is a condition that can improve with the right medical or therapeutic help from professionals. There is always hope.

Trying to Enjoy When They Excel or Are Having a "Good Day"

What happens when your friend, sibling, or whoever is having a really good day? How do you respond to that? What is your reaction? Are you positive and encouraging? Perhaps it's hard for you not to hold your breath and wait for the other shoe to drop, so to speak. What I mean is that you are so used to being in crisis mode so much of the time, that you have a hard time accepting that your friend can actually have a good day, or even a good couple of hours. This is something you should just take at face value and celebrate.

You don't need to point it out to him or make a huge deal out of it; simply enjoy it. Maybe you could suggest doing something together like going to the mall, a pool, ice skating, the movies—whatever you normally do together for fun. It might be the first of many good days to come, so just exhale and be happy for the good times you are able to share.

HEALTHY COPING MECHANISMS

Make a Plan: Battling Your Depression Daily

When you just don't feel right—you're sad, lethargic, or just plain uninterested in anything life has to offer—you need to make a plan. Plan to battle your struggles with depression daily. This chapter will focus on healthy alternatives to letting your depression run your life.

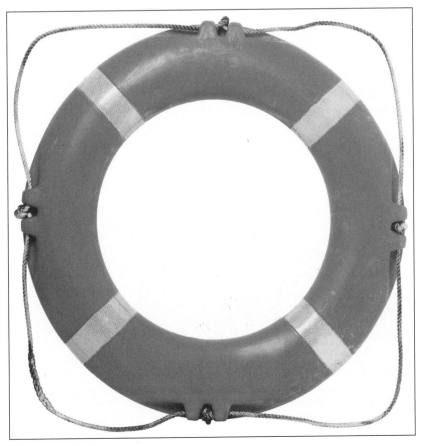

Using your lifelines.

"Reading a truly good fantasy book can take you into another world and away from the reality that we may not be enjoying. Also I recommend the website/blog www.tumblr.com, as well as the book "Thirteen Reasons Why" by Jay Asher. Lastly, when people are depressed they think that nobody is there for them, when really so many are there that they just don't see. If someone so much as made a Facebook status saying how they feel or why they're sad, I can guarantee that so many people that they never knew cared about them actually do. Somebody is always going to be there [to comment]."—Kathryn, age 14[a]

Short-Term Goals

Sometimes lists can make a person feel better. Being able to check things off a list, then look at all you've accomplished in a day can give you a sense of accomplishment. But when you're in a depressive state, just writing a list can be way too much to ask of you. Therefore, let's start with a few minor short-term goals to help get you started and motivate you.

Begin by setting a time of day that you'd like to wake up. Does anyone really like to wake up in the morning and get out of a nice, warm bed? Probably not, but then again, some (nondepressed) people are really excited to start their days!

"When I was young, I had two songs I would play over and over again for hours. They were my sad songs and since all I knew to do back then was cry when no one was watching, I would play those and cry because I felt that no one understood me. I have always done journaling. Before I used it as a venting thing since I was always hiding the way I felt, but it would often turn negative or into suicide notes. I am currently working on a fun journal which I am filling with things I love (drawings of Sponge Bob Square Pants, drawings of squirrels, etc.) things to cheer me up (stickers, perfume samples, fun tattoos) and when I need to vent I will do it in the form of a CBT [Cognitive Behavioral Therapy] sheet so that it helps me rather than leading to a [downward] spiral."—Susan, age 20[b]

Let's help you become one of those people. The following is a list of things you can put on your short-term list of things to aspire to. If you can do one or two of these things over the next few weeks, then good for you!

- Get out of bed by 7:00 a.m. every day for a week.
- Take a shower *and* brush your teeth three days in a row.
- Make it to school or work for a *full* week without calling in sick.
- Call Depression Bipolar Support Alliance (DBSA).
- Find a local support group through DBSA or by googling "Depression Support Groups + [your zip code]"
- Confide your true feelings of depression to one person.
- Have at least one conversation in a day, even if it's with a stranger at the grocery store.

Long-Term Goals

Once you've got a handle on some short-term goals, set your sights further on the horizon. Let's set some long-term goals now. If you can just do one of these things every few months, consider yourself successful!

- Finish one semester of high school or college (eventually leading up to graduation).
- Call a local community college about training for a job (i.e., cosmetology, automotive repair, carpentry, etc.).
- Get a part-time job (even if only earning minimum wage); seek out a low stress atmosphere.
- Volunteer at places like a soup kitchen, a church, a synagogue, or a mosque.
- Build or rebuild a relationship with a friend or family member.
- Learn a new skill/try doing a project (a craft, music, writing, etc.).

Creative Outlets: Journaling, Poetry, Artwork, and Photography

I know I'm not the first person in the world to turn to writing and/or journaling to help make myself feel better. And you know that you aren't the first teen to do it either. All sorts of emotions are released while writing. You may find it to be a cathartic experience. You can also read many books by teens that were written during depressed times, tough times, and happy times.

Have you ever noticed that there's something about writing that allows you to be more honest and true? It is especially that way when dealing with feelings.

"For me, it's about maintaining a healthy lifestyle. I don't really drink, I quit smoking cigarettes, I try (sometimes failing) to eat healthy, and exercise is key to my mental health. My dad always said a sound body makes a sound mind, and I agree with him."—Deb, adult reflecting back on her early 20s[c]

If you've never tried to write something, take out some paper or your laptop now. I'm not asking for a wondrous poem, or song lyrics, or something "magical" to happen—at least not magical on the grand scale of the universe. However, something magical might just happen for you! You might be able to open up about feelings you can't really share or even explain to someone else. That's the kind of gift writing can be for some people.

Maybe the words don't come to you, but you can sure doodle, sketch, and draw out your feelings well. Try to sketch something intangible, such as a feeling. What does *mad* look like? How about a picture of *scared*? Can you sketch that, too, or take a photograph? Then there are things like *happy*, *excited*, and most importantly—*hopeful*! What would a word like *hopeful* look like to you? You'd be amazed at how different each person's interpretation looks.

Hobbies such as photography, writing, drawing, sports, or acting can draw you out of a funk if you immerse yourself in the activities. Give one a try! *Photo courtesy of Heather Schwartz*

Two Books Written by Teens for Teens

Chicken Soup for the Teen Soul: Real-Life Stories by Real Teens, edited by Jack Canfield, Mark Victor Hansen, and Stephanie H. Meyer (New York: Health Communications, Inc., 2007).

Struggle to Be Strong: True Stories by Teens about Overcoming Tough Times, edited by Al Desetta and Sybil Wolin (Minneapolis, MN: Free Spirit Publishing, 2000).

These teen writers share a range of emotions that would be hard to share in person. Writing empowered the teen authors by giving them a voice, and you can get that same feeling by writing, if you choose to give it a try.

There are so many things that "the arts" can give to teens. That's why adults get so upset when schools threaten to cut programming in schools. The arts are important to children and teens, too, not just adults! Music, dance, writing, art, photography, movies, stage plays—the list of "the arts" is lengthy. When you experience the arts, you will often get something out of it. The performance of a certain ballet, for example, or an opera, can move someone to tears with its raw emotion. But I'd argue the point that the artist/performer gets even more out of the arts through creation!

If you've never played a note of music, or sewn a stitch of clothing, or written a single sentence, do yourself a favor . . . try it. Try something very different than what you are used to doing. I'm certain you will get something out of it, and if not, try another thing until you've found a new interest.

Breathing Techniques

One of the most helpful ways to immediately deal with anxiety and depression can be breathing techniques. The book *When Nothing Matters Anymore: A Survival Guide for Depressed Teens*, by Bev Cobain, RN, C, has a great section about breathing that teaches you how to do specific techniques. Some highlights are:

- Pick a place where you can be comfortable and uninterrupted.
- Relax, but don't get so relaxed that you fall asleep.

- Sit or lie down, whichever is most comfortable without being too comfortable to stay awake.
- Feel yourself breathe, concentrating on the in and out movements of your body.
- If you have trouble relaxing, try tensing each part of the body, one at a time, and then relaxing each part, as well. For example, make a fist of each hand, hold it for five seconds while you take a breath and release it, and then relax your hands. You can do this with your face, shoulders, stomach, feet, and so on.
- As you continue with the tensing and relaxing of your whole body, your breathing will get deeper, and you will become more aware of it. The experience should be a pleasant one.[1]

Relaxing is not always as easy as it sounds. When you're wound up, trying to clear your mind and concentrate on your breathing might be a large undertaking. Be patient with yourself, and take your time. You might have to stop and start again several times. Get up, move around, take a break, then you can lie down and try all over again. It should be a soothing feeling, so if it makes you more anxious, simply try again in a few minutes. Deep breathing should make you feel calm and centered.

Cognitive Behavioral Therapy

Cognitive behavioral therapy is a way to change your negative thinking and behaviors. Since a big part of depression can involve negative inner thoughts, you may need to work on ways to train yourself to think more positively. That can be hard to do when you're depressed. Your self-esteem may be low right now. Perhaps you feel like you don't do anything right, or you don't look right, or you just plain don't feel right. There are techniques to cope with these feelings. One way is to perform daily affirmations.

Daily Affirmations

Since a large part of depression can manifest as negative self-talk, practicing what I'll call "daily affirmations" can be a way to reset your thinking and self-image.

There was a television skit that aired in 1991 on TV's *Saturday Night Live*. A character named Stuart Smalley practiced affirmations in the mirror, ending each skit with the phrases, "I'm good enough, I'm smart enough, and doggone it, people like me!" While his mannerisms and facial expressions were funny, there was some real truth in the benefits of practicing such affirmations.

Here's one way to do an affirmation. Take a part of yourself that you feel uncertain about, say your intelligence. If you're doing poorly in school, you can pump yourself up by saying (out loud) to yourself, "I will do my homework today," or "If I don't understand the assignment, I *will* ask the teacher for help before I go home, so I can complete the assignment on time."

Perhaps you don't like a feature of your appearance; maybe you think you're too short. An affirmation might be, "I am just the right size for me. I have a healthy, strong body that I will take care of by getting rest each night."

Another negative self-talk might be that you are overweight. While that might be a daily struggle, you can still make a daily affirmation. "I am a good person, and am beautiful both inside and out." People come in all shapes and sizes, so accept where you are right now in your life.

If your weight is a health concern, just take it one day, or one task at a time. For example, make an effort to walk around the block one time. See how you feel. Then you can try it again tomorrow and the next day. Before you know it, your daily affirmation might be, "I am making stronger efforts to take care of my body each day, and I'm doing a great job!"

The most important part of daily affirmations is to take a positive look at yourself. Even if you are in a bad place right now, and even if you have issues with self-loathing, *try* to see what's good in you. Everyone has positives about themselves, and you might have to look hard sometimes to feel it. There are many wonderful things about you, whether you can admit it out loud to yourself or not. Here's a list of things you can review, and I'm sure you will see yourself in some of them:

I am a nice person.
I am a good son or daughter.
I am a good friend.
I am a good sister or brother.
I am a good listener.
I have a generous spirit.
I can ride a bike.
I can draw well.
I can take beautiful photographs.
I am good at sports.
I am a good speller.
I am good at math.
I am a good person.

Yoga and Meditation

Yoga seems like an easy form of exercise, but in truth, it can be difficult at first. It involves balance, stretching, and coordination. Other parts of yoga are breathing techniques and meditation.

At your local YMCA or community center, yoga classes may be offered. You might not be able to do the poses right away, but you can start small and move on from there. For example, you might want to be able to do a standard pose such as the downward dog, where you place your hands and feet several feet apart, with your butt up in the air, making a triangle out of your body. (It's almost like doing a push up, but you push your bottom toward the ceiling.) This will make good use of your upper body and calf muscles, although you may not have enough strength when you begin doing this pose.

Another goal you might have is to be able to touch your toes with your fingers. This is something that might take several sessions to achieve, but if you stretch each and every day, you'll get closer and closer until you can finally touch them!

Yoga is meant to help relax the mind, body, and spirit. Do yourself a favor, and give it a try!

Exercise

Sports are another healthy way to blow off steam when you're feeling upset or maybe not feeling anything as the case may be with your depression. You've probably heard the word *endorphins* at one point in time. Endorphins are chemicals released in the body when anxiety or a certain physical threshold has been reached, usually by exercising. Some runners get an "endorphin high" when they do a lot of exercise. It is often described as a good feeling.

Taking care of your body is one way to get "on track" for an overall healthier you. When your body is feeling good, your spirits can be lifted naturally as well.

More Helpful Books

Two books you may find helpful are *Breathe: Yoga for Teens*, by Mary Kaye Chryssicas (New York: DK Publishing, 2007), and *Overcoming Trauma through Yoga: Reclaiming Your Body*, by David Emerson (Berkeley, CA: North Atlantic Books, 2011).

"Walking helps me burn off some of my negative emotions. It takes that adrenaline rush to hate and fight and does something good with it. Walking also helps me clear my head. I walk until I can't walk anymore."

—Tamara Ballard, written at age 16[d]

You can do something as simple as walking or running, or play some organized sports at school or at your local recreational center. A game of basketball might help get the blood pumping through your body and give you a little pick-me-up. Your circulation, muscles, and breathing will all improve with activity. Plus, you might make some new friends in the meantime. Having a shared hobby, such as sports, is a great way to break the ice when meeting new people.

Finding (and Trusting) a Nonprofessional to Confide In

You've done it; you've said it out loud to yourself or even taken an online assessment test to see if you are what we'll call clinically depressed. Yes. The answer is yes, you are. Now what? Before getting overwhelmed and letting the inner voice of hopelessness creep in, take a deep breath. There are people and places to turn to for help, even if you are still young and are feeling a bit helpless. Here's a list of people you might turn to first:

1. Your parent(s)
2. An adult family member (stepparent, grandparent, aunt, or uncle)
3. A family member who is a peer (sibling, cousin, stepbrother or stepsister)
4. A teacher
5. The school nurse
6. Your school's guidance counselor
7. A friend's parent (if you feel especially close to him or her)
8. A neighbor
9. Your priest, rabbi, or other clergyman
10. The local pharmacist (he or she can probably at least give you some literature or an 800 number to call for advice)

It sounds obvious to talk to someone you're close to, but sometimes that can be scary. You might worry about how he will react to hearing your feelings. And if he doesn't know the exact right thing to say, cut him some slack. I'm sure he will feel relieved that you confided in him and will want to do the best thing possible to help you.

If confiding in someone you love truly is too daunting, then start with someone objective who may or may not know you that well, such as your doctor, pharmacist, or even a clergyman. Sometimes speaking to someone with no real knowledge of how you were before or have been lately is just what you need—an objective listener.

Admitting you need help is the first real step you can take.

Support Groups

The biggest hurdle you may encounter as a young adult dealing with depression is taking that first step and looking at yourself, your behaviors, and your feelings honestly. Could you really be clinically depressed? And if so, who can you turn to for help? This is a time where you might consider a support group. You can google local social workers in your area and call to see if any of them facilitate support groups.

Support groups help in a number of ways. One thing is that you can open up with strangers because they have no preconceived notions about you and your story. They can listen objectively and share thoughts and feelings that might be similar. They can even give suggestions as to what has helped them in similar situations. There is something freeing about hearing an objective opinion. Also, a support group will show you that you are not alone, and you aren't the only one to have the feelings you may be having.

One of the most well-known support groups is one called Al-Anon, and it is for people who love someone with an addiction. (Alcoholics Anonymous, or AA, is the group that treats the addict.) If your parent or sibling is an alcoholic or drug addict, you might find just the right support from a group like Al-Anon, or one specifically for young people called Alateen. These groups are specifically set up for *loved ones* of those with addictions, *not* necessarily for the addicted person. It is an anonymous group so when you share your feelings or situation, it is to stay within the group, as a safe and nurturing environment. For example, you would be known to the group as "Cheryl R." to protect your privacy. No last names are ever used, just your first name and last initial. You don't even really need to use your real name if you're truly feeling super-private. Groups such as Al-Anon or Alateen are usually held at a church or a school or some other public building. You can find a local support group near you on the Internet by going to www.al-anon. alateen.org/local-meetings. This website helps people to find meetings in the United States, Canada, Bermuda, and Puerto Rico. You can also call 1-888-4AL-ANON (1-888-425-2666) for more information.

Al-Anon members are not there to give advice to other members. The point is to share personal experiences and stories. Sometimes sharing one's own problems can be a cathartic experience. Saying what is bothering you out loud can give

Teens Share Why They Came to Alateen

Girl: "When I went there I was like, 'Eew, I don't want to go,' and then after I started to go, I loved it. I met all these great people and I can talk about all of my feelings now . . . they don't judge you here."

Boy: "I got started when a social worker had taken me to Alateen. I was just thinking, 'It's just another counseling session. I've been to a hundred of them,' but after listening two or three times, it began to stick. . . . So much of it is your mindset, and how you can change it. Alateen has helped me with that."[e]

clarity to your problems. And oftentimes, it helps to say things out loud and realize that they truly aren't as horrible as they seem in your head. Not to mention the fact that hearing others who may be experiencing the same problems could provide a comfort to you, knowing you are not alone in your experiences. One of the sayings in AA and Al-Anon is "Take what you like and leave the rest," which means that if you like someone's sharing, use it to help your own situation. If you disagree or do not like what someone shared, simply forget about it!

Professional Psychotherapy— What Can Each Specialist Do for Me?

If you're not ready to share your feelings with a group, you might want to consider having private counseling sessions with a licensed therapist, counselor, psychiatrist, or social worker. Having an objective person help you navigate your feelings without being judgmental can be very liberating. It helps to feel like someone understands you and what you are going through, along with knowing someone is "on your side." (When paired with other treatments such as medication, the success can be elevated even more.) But how do you know which person to contact? Here is a list of what each person is trained to do:

- Psychiatrists—Psychiatrists are medical doctors (MDs) who have been trained in mental health disorders. They are permitted to prescribe medication, order laboratory tests, and conduct assessments and evaluations to see if you have any mental disorders. These doctors would oversee your care in determining if medication is necessary, determining what and how much is necessary for you to take, and adjusting the medication if it's not working properly.[2]

- Family doctors—Some family doctors are trained in psychotherapy and can prescribe medications and provide counseling.[3]
- Clinical psychologists—These people have an advanced degree in psychology (PhD or PsyD), and they are able to treat emotional and behavioral disorders through various psychotherapies. However, they cannot prescribe medication. They can only test, diagnose, and treat the disorders psychologically.[4]
- Clinical social workers—These people have a master's degree in social work called a MSW. They are trained in diagnosing and treating emotional disorders such as depression, anxiety, bipolar, and other disorders, often through talk therapy. Many health care facilities, such as schools, family service agencies, private practices, and mental health clinics have a MSW on staff.[5]
- Counselors—There are a variety of counselors depending on the issues they help to treat. For example, addiction counselors help people who abuse alcohol or drugs. Religious counselors are often trained to help people with emotional problems and/or marriage problems. Counselors are trained to do talk therapy, not to prescribe medications. They are often trained to help teens. School counselors usually have a master's degree, helping teens with emotional and educational problems.[6]

Sometimes, when someone first begins to seek counseling, a patient will see the therapist a couple of times per week, and then gradually see the therapist less often. As time goes on, patients might only need to see their therapists every one to three weeks for maintenance. This bimonthly check-in will help a person to focus on the positive and keep his or her depression at bay.

It is important to find just the right therapist for you. It should be someone you feel you can trust, someone you can open up to completely without feeling self-conscious. Sometimes it might take visiting a few different therapists to find just the right one. You can interview the potential therapist with questions that are important to you. For example, can he suggest a support group for other teens with depression? Does she do family therapy if you want to have some sessions with your parents and/or siblings present? Don't be afraid to ask lots of questions, especially about things that are important to you. You will be building a relationship with this person, so ultimately you have to "like" the therapist enough to do some very difficult (sometimes) work together on very emotionally charged issues. Take the time to find just the right person for the job!

Sometimes, insurance will cover private counseling sessions. You, or your parent or guardian, will only be responsible for making what is called a co-payment. Many policies have coverage for what are called clinical syndromes (examples are depression, schizophrenia, social phobia, according to the *Diagnostic and Statistical Manual of Mental Disorders*, fifth edition). These might seem like scary labels to you, but it is worth calling your insurance carrier to investigate coverage. Your health and well-being are worth any price. If your parents don't have the financial resources, don't let that obstacle stop you from seeking the treatment you may need. There are places that work on what is called a sliding scale where you can pay what price you can afford. You just need to call around or search the Internet to find places that work in the mental health field and accept sliding scale payments.

Medication

Since depression is believed, by some, to be linked to a chemical imbalance in the brain, trying to correct it with medication might be the right solution to alleviating the problem. Although you might feel weak or like a failure trying medication, it is nothing to be ashamed of. It is medical intervention for a medical issue.

So what's in the medicine that your doctor wants to prescribe? Most likely, your doctor might prescribe SSRI medication, which stands for selective serotonin reuptake inhibitor—huh? They are medications that help your body prevent the reabsorbing of serotonin into your body.[7]

If your level of serotonin is low, you may become depressed. That's where SSRI medication comes into play. When the body's receptors are damaged or even partially missing, depression can occur. SSRIs help add serotonin back into your brain, where it belongs.[8] (There are other neurotransmitters that may need adjusting, and serotonin is just one of them.)

Some SSRIs are commonly known by their brand names (and generic names in parentheses): Celexa (citalopram), Lexapro (escitalopram), Prozac (fluoxetine), Paxil (paroxetine), and Zoloft (sertaline).

How Can Antidepressants Help?

Antidepressants can

- improve mood,
- relieve physical symptoms like fatigue and insomnia,
- create feelings of calmness and stability, and
- decrease the number of irrationally hopeless thoughts.[9]

Medications—It May Take a Few Tries to Get the Right Fit for You

According to the largest national study of depression, commonly referred to as STAR*D, 70 percent of people did not respond to the first antidepressant prescribed for them.[f] (STAR*D stands for Sequenced Treatment Alternatives to Relieve Depression, and is funded by the National Institute of Mental Health. You can learn more by going to www.star-d.org, or by going to http://www.nimh.nih.gov/funding/clinical-trials-for-researchers/practical/stard/index.shtml.)

In the past, there were two other types of antidepressants more commonly prescribed. One was monoamine oxidase inhibitors (MAOIs) and the other was tricyclic antidepressants. While they are still (rarely) prescribed today, those drugs seem to have dangerous interactions with other medications.[10] Also, they are believed to have much more serious side effects for patients.[11]

According to Dr. Purvi Vyas, PharmD, a pharmacist in Grayslake, Illinois, MAOIs interact with any foods with tryptophan, such as cheese and other dairy products, chocolate, eggs, fish, or poultry, and can cause hypertensive crisis (very high blood pressure). (Tryptophan is an amino acid needed for normal growth in infants and for nitrogen balance in adults. It is an essential amino acid, which

Black Box Warning

"In 2004, a FDA advisory committee reviewed data on the safety and effectiveness of antidepressant medications," according to a 2010 National Alliance on Mental Illness report. The study discovered that 1.7 percent of their trial participants (receiving antidepressant medications) experienced suicidal thoughts or engaged in some form of suicidal behavior. There were no suicides in any of the clinical trials, but based on these findings, they gathered that approximately 2 out of 100 children on these medications may experience symptoms of suicidal tendencies in the beginning weeks of starting the medications. That is why the "black box warning" went into effect and was placed on the medication packaging, as a safety precaution.[9]

means your body cannot produce it—you must get it from your diet.)[12] More commonly prescribed drugs include SSRIs, SNRIs (serotonin-norepinephrine reuptake inhibitors), and dopamine antagonists, which is what it sounds like, a drug that blocks dopamine receptors. The only time Dr. Vyas sees MAOIs prescribed is if nothing else has worked in the past, including multiple other treatments.[13] (Such patients who have not had relief from multiple treatments have what is referred to as treatment resistance.)

There are several questions you may want to ask your doctor before asking for a prescription of drug therapy. Here are some of them:

- If I take an antidepressant, how long will it be before I start feeling better?
- How do I know if it's not working/when it's time to try something else?
- What are the common side effects of taking such a (prescribed) drug?
- Are there certain foods that will react or interact poorly with this drug (such as tryptophan, mentioned earlier)?
- Do my other medications interact with this prescription (such as an ADD prescription)?
- How long will I need to be on this medication?
- What happens if I miss a dose? Should I take two the next time, or just skip it?
- What if I start feeling really badly from taking this medication? I heard suicidal thoughts are possible. How can I watch out for that?

These are all potential questions to get answers to when considering taking a prescription medication.[14] Your doctor should have all the answers you will need. There is no shame in needing medication for your medical issues!

> "Sometimes I wonder if my life wouldn't be such a constant struggle with depression if I got medication or talked to a professional. But secretly, I'm afraid. I can't bring myself to open up and talk with someone, like I've failed myself in some way . . . that it will make me less of a person, and weak to hide behind medication. My 'coping' methods seem to veer on the side of denial. Filling out this questionnaire makes me wonder if maybe it's time to reach out and get help. I spend so much of my time just trying to function like a 'normal' person, that I don't have energy for school or a decent job. I want to be a better person, but am struggling in all aspects of my life. Hopefully this book will make others in my position realize they could be more, do more, if they reach out and get help!"—Veronica, early 20s[h]

Electroconvulsive Therapy

Formerly known as "shock therapy," electroconvulsive therapy (ECT) used to have a bad reputation. But when medication and/or psychotherapy are not proving helpful, this form of therapy has been useful to provide relief for people with severe depression.[15] ECT is considered one of the most effective methods to alleviate major depression that has been treatment resistant and requires urgent attention.[16]

What is ECT, exactly? Developed in 1938, this is a technique that uses low-voltage electrical stimulation of the brain. It is administered for a few seconds to patients under anesthesia.[17] The purpose is to treat forms of major depression, anxiety, acute mania, and schizophrenia. Essentially, the electrical currents that are sent through the brain cause a brief seizure, which affects signal pathways and neurotransmitters in the brain. It reduces the severity of depression.[18] It could potentially save a life, although the treatment is still thought of as highly controversial by some.[19] People who cannot take antidepressant drugs, or have not responded fully to antidepressant drugs are potential candidates for this procedure, as well as people who are suicidal.[20]

Risks Associated with ECT

Since the dose of electricity used in the ECT procedure has been greatly reduced, the side effects have been reduced as well. However, the treatment can still cause some, including

- confusion that generally lasts for only a short period of time,
- headache,
- low blood pressure or high blood pressure,
- memory loss,
- muscle soreness,
- nausea, and
- rapid heartbeat or other heart problems.[21]

Some medical conditions put patients at greater risk for side effects from ECT. That's why it's imperative to discuss any concerns with your doctor when deciding whether it is a viable and safe treatment option for you.

Natural Alternatives to Help with Depression

Perhaps taking medications or having invasive therapies such as ECT is too drastic of a step for you right now. You may be very in tune with your body and not want

A New Therapy for Depression Called tDCS

There is an inexpensive treatment that is being tested now that could potentially complement existing medication. It is transcranial direct current stimulation (tDCS). It is intended for people who cannot take medication or are not completely helped by it. It can be used instead of medication or taken in tandem with it.

According to information on the website www.transcranialbrainstimulation .com, tDCS is easy to do. Moist sponge electrodes are placed on the scalp and held in place with an elastic headband, overlying the targeted areas of the brain. There is no perceptible sensation or only a slight tingling under the electrode. The patient is comfortably sitting or lying down.

Dr. James Fugedy, an anesthesiologist in Atlanta, Georgia, who educates people on the risks and benefits of tDCS, has treated patients for over thirty years. He graduated from the Creighton University School of Medicine, completed his residency in anesthesiology at the Yale–New Haven Hospital, and was certified by the American Board of Anesthesiology.

Dr. Fugedy says, "For treatment-resistant conditions, listening to the patient is especially important. The most profound insights often come from the patient's own words. Communication forms the foundation of the therapeutic relationship upon which healing occurs."[i]

He goes on to say,

When I read the initial studies utilizing transcranial direct current stimulation, I was very excited because here was a procedure for treatment-resistant chronic pain patients which was effective, easy-to-do, inexpensive and without side effects.

Currently, I provide tDCS for treatment-resistant patients suffering from the chronic, central pain syndromes, . . . depression, and tinnitus. tDCS also demonstrates benefit for stroke rehabilitation. In the future, I envision tDCS providing benefit for ADD and autism patients, as well as for enhancing memory and learning.[j]

to subject it to traditional medication and treatments, but you might try some natural alternatives *in addition* to other therapies. (However, always tell your doctor first, if you want to add something to your prescribed regimen.)

Healthy nutrition can help with emotional moods, along with your overall physical well-being. In America, oftentimes it is easier, and cheaper, to just grab fast food. This isn't going to improve your overall health or moods though. It is essential to try and eat right.

As a side note, caffeine is a drug that is best avoided when dealing with depression. Caffeine withdrawal is often associated with headaches, fatigue, depression, anxiety, and drowsiness. However, these characteristics usually go away within forty-eight hours, or when the person has caffeine again.[22] Still, it's best to err on the side of caution, and avoid things high in caffeine such as coffee, some tea, and many sodas. With so many sleep disorders prevalent in depression, caffeine might aggravate those symptoms of sleeplessness and restlessness all the more.

While ginseng, ginkgo biloba, and St. John's wort are common home remedies, Dr. Purvi Vyas, PharmD, says that there has not been sufficient clinical evidence to professionally recommend these things to help with depression.[23]

Alternative Schools and Therapy Programs

There are a variety of treatment facilities that help teens. There are programs for those battling addictions and schools to assist teens with emotional or behavioral problems. Most of these schools are in-patient residential programs where the teens stay overnight anywhere from eight weeks to twelve months.

Some schools use wilderness programs, outdoor education, ranch environments with equestrian therapy, and Outward Bound–type therapies to help the teen address issues within the family or simply inside of one's life.

Fun or Silly Ways to Help Alleviate Your Depression Symptoms

Interact with your family unit as you may have when you were little. Try to play games like Mad Libs, Monopoly, Pictionary, or some other board game. Doodle or sketch, or use chalkboard paint on your bedroom wall. Play with animals.

Groups range from five students to seventy students, mostly kids who struggle in the school environment. The goal is to get them back on track with academics. The teens move at their own pace with the help of teachers and tutors. There can be dual enrollment with high school- and college-credit courses.

The majority of the states that have such schools mandate that the teens cannot check themselves out—the parents have to do that. These states include Utah, Louisiana, South Carolina, and Nevada, to name a few.

As of 2014, the average stay at an in-patient facility costs from $3,995 to $5,000 per month with sixty-day to twelve-month programs available. There is also an enrollment fee that ranges from $3,500 to $6,000, above and beyond the monthly tuition. While some facilities offer monthly payment plans, many families choose to get sponsors for their students, especially for nonprofit schools. Local businesses can donate to the school specifically for one student.[24]

SUCCESS STORIES: YOUNG ADULTS WHO BATTLE DEPRESSION SUCCESSFULLY

How to Come Out of Your Own Depression

This book was intended to help you see that depression, while often chronic, can be managed. You can try a range of therapies from diet and exercise, to vitamins and breathing exercises, to psychotherapy, medication, and even electroconvulsive therapy, if necessary. But what better way to show you that this is a hurdle you can overcome than to share success stories from teens who have been exactly where you are now. They have come out of it on the other side of deep, dark depressive episodes and lived to tell about it.

Success Stories

Each of the following success stories is told in the individual's own words.

Susan, Age 20

After spending what feels like a majority of my life battling with depression, I finally feel one in my thought, word, and deed. Seeing as I am only 20, I realize the road ahead is still long, yet for once I don't feel as daunted by the trek.

It all started in such a simple way—in second grade my best friend's family was deported. Being only seven years old, I was heartbroken and confused. What did deportation even mean? She hadn't died, yet she had moved to an entirely

A series of success stories of young adults, such as Susan, age 20, coping with depression. *Photo courtesy of Maren Lindsay Newman*

different country across the globe, and to a seven-year-old, the two seemed pretty much the same.

After my friend's deportation, life went on, in an almost roller coaster fashion. It was filled with its ups, and with what seemed to be too many downs. I always wanted to be happy, and I spent years trying every method to get there. When I was a junior in high school I ate healthy, exercised almost every day, got plenty of fresh air, proper sleep, took my vitamins, and excelled at school. Problem was, I still had yet to feel happy. Fast forward to my sophomore year of college, and I am attending the number one school for my dream career, which happens to be located in one of the most picturesque cities I have ever encountered. I am finally living in an apartment with my own room, and am on what seems to be a good balance of depression medication. I have even reconnected with my first and only love from high school, who ended up moving out to be with me. Written down, I had it all, yet again, I found myself unhappy.

Junior year of college, my boyfriend and I move into an apartment of our own. For the first time in my life, my schooling was falling behind, and I felt I had tried everything to make my life work. I even had a therapist whom I found deeply helpful, yet I had no inner peace.

Being type A, mixed with an addictive personality, led to many years in fast-forward. I liked the essence of life—I just didn't like being weighed down by all of its struggles. I forgot how to enjoy the journey, and became too affixed on the destination. If you find yourself in a similar manner, the answer is to just stop, and breathe.

After living in dorms for five years, my boyfriend's and my new apartment gave me something I had been lacking. I finally had a spare room, a place I could shut the doors and sit uninterrupted and alone, in peace. I no longer had an excuse to withhold from meditating. Sitting, motionless, in silence, with myself, if I couldn't do that, then how could I believe in myself when it came to more difficult matters.

Meditating can mean something different to us all, but the importance I got from it was taking the time to stop, and rest the body, in order to allow the mind to de-clutter and work through itself. When I first began meditating, I would listen to different mediation videos on YouTube and aimed to do five to fifteen minutes of meditation each day. When you think about it, sitting down and doing absolutely nothing for five to fifteen minutes should be easy; little kids in time outs do it all the time. Not as easy as I expected, I can confess to wiggling my way through many meditations in my early days. The important thing is I did them. They were short bits of nothingness but wow what an impact that nothing created.

I have now been meditating on and off for about seven months. For the first time in my life, I can breathe easy, I can sit without having to constantly distract my mind, I can enjoy the wind against my cheek, the sun on my back, and life is good. Meditation brought me peace, in ways I never thought possible. It allowed me to forgive, myself as well as others, and to realize that there really is a balance of good and bad in the world, and to have it any other way, would make the world lopsided. A wonderful tool I found to help keep me motivated in mediating is called HEADSPACE. It was developed by a Buddhist monk, comes with great animations to help you understand it, and is not biased toward any religion. I am now doing twenty-minute meditations almost daily, and I know weeks I do it daily versus weeks I maybe only do it once, have far different outcomes. Now if you slightly cringe or even giggle at the idea of meditation, I do understand it can sound a bit wacky. But, if you can look past the word, to the idea of sitting for a short time and doing absolutely nothing, then maybe you'll see it can't hurt. It really is a simple task, but one that can calm the mind in ways we all have innate in us. We are all in different life situations, each with our own problems, but one thing we all have in common is our breath. Everyone breathes, and when we each take the time to allow our bodies to get in touch with our breaths, we can more easily find our places in the current of life. If all that was standing in the way of you and true happiness was a little nothingness, wouldn't you at least try?

I spent years worried I would never be happy. I believed since I had some unfavorable childhood memories, my whole life would be sad. I lost sight of the silver lining. While I believe meditation was the cherry on top that finally allowed me to heal, meditation has also reminded me how important balance is. I am now off all my depression medications, and have allowed my body to get in touch with its natural balance. It is hard to be happy, if you are starving, just as it is hard to be happy when you have lost a dear friend. Taking care of all parts of you is important, and that includes the mind. HEADSPACE helped me do that, which then allowed other parts of my life to finally fall into place. HEADSPACE gave me happiness because I now know, no matter where I go, I bring with me my inner peace, almost like an inner oasis, I can escape to anytime I want.[1]

Seth, Age 22

I never experienced depression until I turned 16. Being at a school where I didn't feel very welcome and feeling really alone all the time was really difficult for me.

Celebrity Success Story: Actor Jim Carrey Fought Depression and Won!

Jim Carrey had to drop out of school in his teens, to take care of his ill mother and his siblings. His family struggled to make ends meet. He had chronic depression throughout his life, even after achieving great success professionally in the movies. Jim turned to the drug Prozac and therapy to help battle the depression.[a] Eventually he was able to get off Prozac, saying in a YouTube interview, "I had to get off. It helped me out of a jam, but it was like [living with] a low level of despair." Carrey said he battles depressive feelings through spirituality. He also said, "I rarely drink coffee. I'm very serious about no alcohol, no drugs. Life is too beautiful."[b]

I often felt very isolated and didn't feel comfortable talking with friends or family at the time. Although changing schools and seeing a therapist helped me, my depression still comes back from time to time, especially when I am in an emotionally stressful situation.

I have gotten much better at managing the depression when it comes up and the episodes don't typically last as long as they did in the past. Therapy was very helpful for me and really made me look at things through an objective lens and understand things better. Although I know my depression will never actually go away, it is definitely comforting to know that, along with a great support group, I now have the tools to help me when things do get tough again.

In terms of my sexuality in relation to depression, I think it definitely played a role in it at least partially. I did get made fun of a good bit starting in 8th grade when it was made public knowledge that I was interested in men (I identified as bisexual at the time). In high school, it got a little easier since there were so many more kids and I could blend in a little better, but there was definitely still some ridicule. My mom was great when I was coming out and never questioned me at all. She was totally supportive so I was really lucky in that aspect. My friends were all supportive, but I didn't have many friends throughout high school and most of my close friends moved my freshman year. Once I transferred schools, I was able to make a great group of friends and that really helped me to get past some of my loneliness.

I did experience some depression though in the aspect that I felt like I was alone romantically throughout high school. I would get really down about the fact that I would be like this forever and it would always just be really hard for me to find a partner and that I would probably be more alone more often than not. While this problem still lingers some now, I don't get depressed about it really and I have learned places to look for support from other gay people and learned how to manage my depression when it does flair up.[2]

In May of 2013, Seth graduated from college, began interviewing for jobs, and was considering going to graduate school.

Bella, Age 18

When I was in Paris last summer visiting my Aunt Lizzy, I got depressed. I really wanted to be there, but it was sort of crazy because back home my dad was going through a divorce.

Because I was sleeping all the time, my aunt took me to the doctor who gave me meds for depression. That was all I needed! (Plus, I go to talk therapy when I'm feeling down.)

So finally I got up and went to work and loved the time I had with my dream job of working in a Paris restaurant! Now I'm graduating [high school] in June 2013 and off to college, with a scholarship, in the fall.[3]

Kathryn, Age 14

I never knew much about depression, even when I was feeling it. The only thing I was for sure of was that it was never going away; I was wrong.

Throughout elementary school I was a perfectly normal little girl. I didn't have many friends, but I had my best friend, Kiley. She was my rock, my everything. She was always there for me when nobody else was. Then we made the transfer into middle school. That's when it started to go downhill, for me at least. The group of "cool" girls liked Kiley; she was funny, she was pretty, and the boys liked her. So they decided to take her from me, and she's not the only one who would leave her best friend to be popular, right?

The entire year of fifth grade the only friends I had were guys, but I didn't mind; they were great. It was hard to see my "supposed" best friend walk in the hallways and ignore me because she was popular now, and I wasn't; I was never going to be. The school year ended and nothing had changed, other than me and Kiley had stopped talking completely; it was too awkward.

That summer, I dyed my hair and put on a bit of makeup. I went into the sixth grade just like that, and all of a sudden, the first day of school, the very girls that took my best friend, wanted me to sit with them at lunch. They told me to sit with them again the next day, and the next, and the next, until we were all close friends. I never knew what being "in" felt like before then, and I loved it. I had a lot of friends in the grade above me. I never knew they'd be the last ones there in the end.

I had a boyfriend for almost year and me being my ignorant, young self, I thought I was in love. When he broke up with me, that group of six girls was all that I had; and they were there. They were there for me when I needed to cry, and talk about anything. I was so sure that I had finally found a group of girls that would never leave my side, and they were popular! That means I was [popular], I finally had somewhere to belong.

They taught me what it took to be like them. I kept dying my hair, I wore more makeup, and I wore the brands of clothes they said were in: Pink, Abercrombie, Gilly Hicks. Everything was going amazingly well; people actually knew who I was! I was on top of the world. Then, for some reason, everybody started to get annoyed with me. I was "posing" off of them. They thought I "wanted to be them." Let me tell you, I never wanted to be somebody that I'm not. I just wanted to be accepted for who I am.

It got so much worse. It seemed to all happen so fast, in one day perhaps. They texted me, called me, posted on my Facebook, calling me all sorts of names and claiming I did all these things that never happened. I kissed a boy? I was a whore. I wore the same color eye shadow as Julia? I was a poser. I tried to defend myself? I was a total bitch. I had only two friends left. My friend Kerry, whom

I had known since kindergarten, but never really got along with until that year. She was amazing, she still is. We were instant best friends once we started talking and never stopped. My friend Katy, a year older, never left my side. She was with me the day the bullying started to happen, and she never left my side. Not even when I was in hysterics, bawling in her room. She always knew just what to say and when to say it. She introduced me to her best friend, Heather, and we instantly clicked. To this day, I've never met anybody so relatable, kind, and down to earth as that girl. Katy and Heather were my very best friends, when I swore I wanted to die, they were the reason I didn't and I could never thank them enough for never leaving me. Even today, they are some of my best friends.

I'll skip ahead to the year of seventh grade, not much of anything eventful went on. The group of girls all apologized to me, but I still wonder if they actually meant it. I think that that year is when I found a comfortable middle of trying to be accepted, and not caring whether people liked me or not, as long as I was being myself.

The year of eighth grade, just last year, wasn't too great. I'm not quite sure why, but I changed so much. I became too obsessed with how I looked, how I acted and what people, that didn't even matter, thought of me. I would never admit it to my parents, but it all got to be too much and I didn't know what else to do.

I saw photos on all sorts of social networks of it [cutting] . . . girls my age, younger, older, saying it made them feel better, so why shouldn't I try it? Why shouldn't I self-harm? I was always too scared to do any actual damage, like the stories I've read and the photos I had seen. Only little "cat scratches," but they were my release. I don't see that as a big thing that went on, because looking back at it now, it was only a stage for a couple of months. The need to do it stopped when I got into, what I think, is fantastic and life-saving music . . . bands like All Time Low, Pierce the Veil, A Day to Remember, and Sleeping with Sirens.

People now think of some of these bands as stereotypical groups that people only listen to, to seem cool. This makes me more upset than anything, because I love them and it's nice to know that the people in these bands have struggled with bullying, self-harm, substance abuse and have come from broken families but they're still here. They did it, they made it through everything and now they're more successful than the ones who ever tried to drag them down.

It [music] is not just a teenage thing like lots of adults seem to think, music saves and changes lives; I wouldn't be the happy person that I am today without it. Now that I am in my freshman year in high school, I know that I'm where I need to be. I know that I don't need everybody's approval to be happy. I know to be happy to anybody who I come across, because who knows what they're going through? I'm happy where I am today.

Of course, sometimes I do still get stressed and upset, because nobody's life is perfect, but there are so many better ways to cope that I now know of. Everybody says "it gets better," which is true. But it'll only get better if you want it to. I had to focus really hard on trying to be positive, and really wanting to be happy again. I've realized that somebody was always there for me, I just never noticed. Looking back, my biggest mistake was caring so much about what people thought of me. I like being able to be completely happy and content with being one hundred percent myself now.[4]

Successful Celebrities: Depression and the Creative Types

Throughout history, many creative types have publicly dealt with depression. It's not to say that all creative people are depressed. However, many public figures have admitted that whether because of it, or despite it, their process of dealing with depression has helped with the creative process. According to Sarah Glynn in an article on www.medicalnewstoday.com, the majority of some psychiatric diseases, such as depression, anxiety syndrome, schizophrenia, and substance abuse, are more prevalent among authors in particular.[5] (It was not stated, however, why that is believed to be true.)

Seven Presidents Who Battled Depression

If you consider that the president of the United States is usually thought of as the most powerful man in the world, then how on earth could that person suffer from depression? Presidents are just like everyone else; depression is something that cannot be helped. It is something certain people just have to deal with. Some of the afflicted presidents were John Adams, Thomas Jefferson, Franklin Pierce, Abraham Lincoln, James Madison, John Quincy Adams, and Calvin Coolidge. Many of these men dealt with death of family members, often their children, and other traumatic events that certainly could have triggered such depressive feelings.[6]

Final Thoughts

Whether your low feelings stem from grief over losing someone, a traumatic event such as rape, coping with a serious illness such as cancer, or perhaps none of these—nothing in particular at all—if you've been feeling down or not like yourself for more than two weeks and you can't just snap out of it as some may have suggested to you, then you may suffer from depression. It is not your fault! Many people, as you have just read, suffer from depression, and it is not something you need to be ashamed of. My biggest hope in writing this book is that

Successful High-Profile People with Depression

Depression doesn't have to limit what you can achieve. Throughout history, many people have suffered from depression and gone on to lead very successful lives. Here is a list of famous people who achieved professional success, even while suffering from depression.[c]

Joan of Arc, French saint (1412–1431)

Wolfgang Amadeus Mozart, Austrian composer (1756–1791)

John Quincy Adams, American president (1767–1848)

Abraham Lincoln, American president (1809–1865)

Mark Twain, American writer (1835–1910)

Mother Theresa of Calcutta, humanitarian and religious worker (1910–1997)

Audrey Hepburn, British actress (1929–1993)

Dick Clark, American entertainer (1929–2012)

Sir Anthony Hopkins, British actor (1937–)

Harrison Ford, American actor (1942–)

Michael Crichton, American writer (1942–)

Oprah Winfrey, American talk show host (1954–)

Ellen DeGeneres, American comedienne (1958–)

Simon Cowell, British record producer (1959–)

Hugh Laurie, British actor (1959–)

J. K. Rowling, British writer (1965–)

Halle Berry, American actress (1966-)

Mike Tyson, American boxer (1966–)

Queen Latifah, American singer (1970–)

Drew Barrymore, American actress (1975–)

Alicia Keys, American musician (1981–)

Beyoncé Knowles, American singer (1981–)

Lady Gaga, American musician (1986–)

Kellie Pickler, American singer (1986–)

you now feel a little less alone, a little less helpless, and perhaps not hopeless at all any more. There *is* hope. Reread sections of this text if necessary to remind yourself of small ways to help you cope. Go to the index to refresh your memory of something you may have found helpful, such as breathing techniques, or hobbies to express yourself such as writing, reading, photography, dance, sports, and so on. Take a look at the recommended reading section. There are several suggestions throughout this book to help you to keep on making it through another day.

No matter where you are on your depression journey, you are in charge and can chart your own destiny. Things don't have to end badly. There are many places to turn to and many professional people equipped to help you write your own success story. The key thing to always remember is to hang in there, ask for help, and don't give up!

Glossary

anorexia nervosa:an eating disorder where a person's self-perception is altered to where he or she feels grossly overweight, even if at a dangerously low weight. People with anorexia nervosa often obsess about their weight and the food they've eaten.

antidepressants:drugs used to relieve symptoms associated with depression or sometimes other mood disorders.

bipolar disorder:often characterized by periods of mania and depression, and can be accompanied by periods of normal moods, too. It is characterized by cycling mood changes.

bulimia:eating disorder where a person frequently eats an abnormally large quantity of food (binges) then feels compelled to purge it via self-induced vomiting or the use of laxatives.

bullying:the act of badgering or intimidating someone repeatedly.

cognitive behavioral therapy (CBT):type of psychotherapy where the goal is to examine the relationship between thoughts, feelings, and behaviors by redirecting negative thought patterns that produce unwanted behavior; used to treat mood disorders such as depression.

Department of Children and Family Services (DCFS):government organization to protect children from abuse and neglect. (Similar organizations are throughout the country in every state.)

depression:mood disorder where feelings of hopelessness and inadequacy last for more than two weeks.

dysthemia:type of low-grade depression that is persistent, often lasting two years or longer. While it does not disable a person, it may prevent normal functioning or feeling well.

electroconvulsive therapy (ECT):also known as shock therapy; a treatment where electric currents are passed through the brain to trigger a brief seizure. It is used to relieve certain mental illnesses such as depression.

hoarding:disorder where a person has trouble organizing and being able to throw things away, amassing large quantities of objects. Affected people are often burdened with health risks, economic troubles, and shame.

insomnia:sleep disorder where people have trouble falling asleep or staying asleep for more than a few hours at a time.

major depressive disorder:mental disorder that causes a loss of interest in things previously enjoyed, and is accompanied by a persistent low mood. It affects a person's ability to work, sleep, study, or eat. Some people may only experience a single episode within their lifetime, but it is common for a person to have multiple episodes.

monoamine oxidase inhibitor (MAOI):the first type of antidepressant developed.

neurotransmitters:chemicals in the brain responsible for communication between brain cells. They carry information from one neuron to another.

obsessive-compulsive disorder (OCD):condition affecting the brain and behavior, causing severe anxiety with thoughts, images, or impulses that occur over and over again producing an "out of control" sensation. Repetitive actions, which people engage in to try and make feelings go away, usually interfere with daily life and productivity.

postpartum depression (PPD):low mood many women experience after giving birth, during hormonal and physical changes that come along with the stresses of caring for a newborn.

post-traumatic stress disorder (PTSD):develops after going through a traumatic experience where the person witnesses physical harm or the threat of physical harm. The harm may have happened to them or to a loved one.

premenstrual dysphoric disorder (PMDD):severe form of premenstrual syndrome where a woman has severe depression symptoms, irritability, and tension before menstruation. There is a list of symptoms of which five or more must be present to diagnose PMDD; however there is no physical exam or lab test to diagnose it.

psychotherapy:talk therapy with a counselor, therapist, psychologist, or psychiatrist.

seasonal affected disorder (SAD):a disorder that's usual onset comes during the winter months when there is less sunlight. The depression usually lifts during spring and summer.

selective serotonin reuptake inhibitor (SSRI):compound typically used in antidepressants in the treatment of depression, anxiety disorders, and some personality disorders.

self-injuring:act of injuring oneself, usually alone, by cutting, burning, picking, trichotillomania, head banging, or other forms of inducing pain or injury to self.

self-medicating:the use of alcohol, illegal or prescription drugs, or other addictive behaviors such as eating or gambling, to compensate for underlying problems that have not been addressed or treated.

serotonin:naturally occurring chemical in the brain, known as a neurotransmitter, partially responsible for brain functions such as mood, appetite, sleep, and memory.

stigma:negative and often unfair belief regarding a particular situation, group, or person.

substance abuse:chemical dependence on addictive substances such as alcohol or drugs

suicide:the act of taking one's own life.

transcranial direct current stimulation (tDCS):form of stimulation targeted externally that uses a constant, low current delivered directly to the brain area of interest with small electrodes placed on the head. Originally developed to help patients with brain injuries and strokes, it is now used to help treatment resistant patients with anxiety and depression.

treatment resistance:when a symptom or disorder is not alleviated by medication or therapies prescribed.

trigger:an event or situation that causes another event or situation to occur.

unhealthy coping mechanism:way of dealing with a problem or situation that is not in one's best interest, such as self-harm or self-medicating.

Notes

Introduction

1. CGS, journal entry.
2. Margaret O. Hyde and Elizabeth H. Forsyth, MD, *Depression: What You Need to Know* (London, England: Franklin Watts, 2002), p. 51.
3. Hyde and Forsyth, *Depression*, p. 51.
4. Author unknown.

Chapter 1

1. Melvyn Lurie, *Depression: Your Questions Answered* (New York: Dorling Kindersley, 2007), p. 10.
2. Lurie, *Depression*, p. 10.
3. Lurie, *Depression*, p. 10.
4. When Your Head Spins, "Checklist for Signs of Depression," www.wordworx.co.nz/depression.html (accessed September 24, 2009).
5. National Institute of Mental Health (NIMH), "Depression," www.nimh.nih.gov/health/topics/depression/index.shtml (accessed August 21, 2013).
6. NIMH, "Dysthymic Disorder among Children," www.nimh.nih.gov/statistics/1dd_child.shtml (accessed March 13, 2014).
7. Pristiq, "Depression Symptoms," www.pristiq.com/depression_symptoms.aspx?PrinterFriendly=TRUE (accessed September 14, 2011).
8. HelpGuide.org, "Teen Depression: A Guide for Parents," www.helpguide.org/mental/depression_teen.htm (accessed March 13, 2014).
9. Paula Anne Ford-Martin and Teresa G. Odle, "The Causes, Symptoms, and Treatments of Depression," in *Perspectives on Diseases and Disorders: Depression*, ed. Jacqueline Langwith (Farmington Hills, MI: Greenhaven Press, 2008), p. 21.
10. Rebecca Rutledge, *The Everything Parent's Guide to Children with Depression* (Avon, MA: Adams Media, 2007), p. 4.
11. Gabriel Cousens, with Mark Mayell, *Depression-Free for Life: An All-Natural, 5-Step Plan to Reclaim Your Zest for Living* (New York: HarperCollins, 2000), p. 5.
12. www.hmc.psu.edu/healthinfo/d/depression.htm (accessed October 6, 2009).
13. Christina M. Mulé, "Why Women Are More Susceptible to Depression: An Explanation for Gender Differences," SAPA Project Test, www.personalityresearch.org/papers/mule.html (accessed June 8, 2011).
14. Mulé, "Why Women Are More Susceptible."
15. Michael J. Martin, *Teen Depression: Diseases and Disorders* (Farmington Hills, MI: Lucent Books, 2005), p. 28.
16. Martin, *Teen Depression*, p. 29.

17. Mulé, "Why Women Are More Susceptible."

18. Carol Fitzpatrick and John Sharry, *Coping with Depression in Young People: A Guide for Parents* (Chichester, West Sussex, England: John Wiley & Sons, 2004), p. 13.

19. NIMH, "How Does Depression Affect Adolescent Girls?" www.nimh.nih.gov/health/publications/women-and-depression-discovering-hope/index.shtml#pub6 (accessed July 13, 2013).

20. E. Calvete and O. Cardenoso, "Gender Differences in Cognitive Vulnerability to Depression and Behavior Problems in Adolescents," *Journal of Abnormal Child Psychology* 33, no. 2 (April 2005): pp. 179–192.

21. Lisa Machoian *The Disappearing Girl—Learning the Language of Teenage Depression* (New York: Plume, Penguin Group, 2006), p. 178.

22. Allen R. Miller, *Teen's Guides: Living with Depression* (New York: Facts on File, 2008), p. 125; Federal Interagency Forum on Child and Family Statistics, *America's Children: Key National Indicators of Well-Being* (Washington, DC: U.S. Government Printing Office, 2013), available at ww.childstats.gov/americaschildren/health4.asp (accessed August 20, 2013).

a. Federal Interagency Forum on Child and Family Statistics, *America's Children: Key National Indicators of Well-Being*, 2013.

b. American Psychiatric Association, *Diagnostic and Statistical Manual of Mental Disorders*, 5th ed. (Arlington, VA: American Psychiatric Association, 2013), pp. 160–61.

c. Prevention Action, "Diagnosing Teen Depression: New Screener May Help Spot the 'missing 70%,'" www.preventionaction.org/research/diagnosing-teen-depression-new-screener-may-help-spot-missing-70/5818 (accessed March 25, 2014).

d. Alexandra Sifferlin, "A Blood Test to Diagnose Depression in Teens?" *Time.com*, healthland.time.com/2012/04/17/a-blood-test-to-diagnose-depression-in-teens/ (accessed March 13, 2014).

e. Kathyrn, e-mailed questionnaire, December 18, 2012.

f. Veronica, in-person questionnaire, July 12, 2013.

g. NIMH, "Depression."

h. Quoted in U.S. Department of Health and Human Services, *Mental Health: Culture, Race, and Ethnicity—A Supplement to Mental Health: A Report of the Surgeon General* (Rockville, MD: U.S. Department of Health and Human Services, Substance Abuse and Mental Health Services Administration, Center for Mental Health Services, 2001), www.ncbi.nlm.nih.gov/books/NBK44246/ (accessed January 20, 2014).

Chapter 2

1. American Psychiatric Association: *Diagnostic and Statistical Manual of Mental Disorders*, 5th ed. (Arlington, VA: American Psychiatric Association, 2013), p. 271.

2. Mark Goulston, "PTSD Treatment in Children," in *Post-Traumatic Stress Disorder*, ed. Carrie Fredericks (Farmington Hills, MI: Greenhaven Press, 2010), p. 39.

3. Goulston, "PTSD Treatment in Children," p. 40.

4. Goulston, "PTSD Treatment in Children," p. 41.

5. Goulston, "PTSD Treatment in Children," pp. 44–45.

6. National Center for Posttraumatic Stress Disorder, "PTSD Treatment in Adults," in *Post-Traumatic Stress Disorder*, ed. Carrie Fredericks (Farmington Hills, MI: Greenhaven Press, 2010), p. 47.

7. Melvyn Lurie, MD, *Depression: Your Questions Answered* (New York: Dorling Kindersley, 2007), p. 58.

8. Sue Flanagan and Patty Morrison, "Does Birth Order Really Matter?" Extension Service West Virginia University, no. WL237, 2007, www.wvu.edu/~exten/infores/pubs/fypubs/WLG_237%20Birth%20Order%20Member.pdf (accessed October 31, 2013).

9. Committee on Public Education, "Media Violence," *Pediatrics* 124, no. 5 (November 2009): 1495, http://pediatrics.aappublications.org/content/108/5/1222.full.pdf+html (accessed June 2, 2014).

10. Committee on Public Education, "Media Violence," p. 1495.

11. Screening for Mental Health, "Online Connections: Middle School Mental Health and the Effects of Social Media," mentalhealthscreening.org/enews/middleschoolsocialmedia.aspx (accessed February 7, 2014).

12. Screening for Mental Health, "Online Connections."

---

a. Samantha R., "The Effects of Stress, *TeenInk.com*, www.teenink.com/nonfiction/academic/article/369465/The-Effects-of-Stress/ (accessed March 28, 2015).

b. Susan, e-mail, April 28, 2013.

c. CGS, e-mail, October 18, 2012.

d. CGS, e-mail, January 10, 2013.

e. Helen Fitzgerald, *The Grieving Teen: A Guide for Teenagers and Their Friends* (New York: Fireside Book, 2000), p. 103.

f. Committee on Public Education, "Media Violence," p. 1496.

g. Committee on Public Education, "Media Violence," p. 1497.

h. Screening for Mental Health, "Online Connections."

i. Roni Caryn Rabin, "Internet Use Tied to Depression in Youths," *New York Times*, August 9, 2010, www.nytimes.com/2010/08/10/health/research/10beha.html (accessed October 31, 2013).

Chapter 3

1. National Institute of Mental Health, "Depression," www.nimh.nih.gov/health/topics/depression/index.shtml?utm_source=BrainLine.orgutm_medium=Twitter (accessed April 1, 2014).

2. Margaret Strock, "Depression Is a Serious Mental Illness," in *Contemporary Issues Companion: Depression*, ed. Emma Carlson Berne (Farmington Hills, MI: Greenhaven Press, 2007), p. 16.

3. American Psychiatric Association, *Diagnostic and Statistical Manual of Mental Disorders*, 5th ed. (Arlington, VA: American Psychiatric Association, 2013), p. 166.

4. Francis Mark Mondimore, MD, *Depression: The Mood Disease*, rev. ed. (Baltimore and London: Johns Hopkins University Press, 1993), p. 125.

5. American Psychiatric Association, *Diagnostic and Statistical Manual*, p. 63.

6. Todd C. Edwards, PhD, Donald L. Patrick, PhD, and Tari D. Topolski, PhD, "Quality of Life of Adolescents with Perceived Disabilities," *Journal of Pediatric Psychology* abstract study, jpepsy.oxfordjournals.org/content/28/4/233.abstract (abstract accepted September 4, 2002; accessed December 4, 2013).

7. Edwards, Patrick, and Topolski, "Quality of Life."

8. Teens Health, "Depression," in *Mental Health Information for Teens: Health Tips about Mental Wellness and Mental Illness*, 2nd ed. (Detroit, MI: Omnigraphics, 2006), pp. 76–77, www.teenshealth.org.

9. Teens Health, "Depression," pp. 76–77.

10. Teens Health, "Depression," pp. 76–77.

11. Teens Health, "Depression," pp. 76–77.

12. Strock, "Depression Is a Serious Mental Illness," p. 16.

13. Paula Anne Ford-Martin and Teresa G. Odle, "The Causes, Symptoms, and Treatments of Depression," in *Perspectives on Diseases and Disorders—Depression*, ed. Jacqueline Langwith (Farmington Hills, MI: Greenhaven Press, 2009), p. 19.

a. Steven, e-mail, March 7, 2014.

b. Anonymous, "I Beat Depression," *TeenInk.com*, www.teenink.com/hot_topics/what_matters/article/566040/I-Beat-Depression/ (accessed March 28, 2014).

Chapter 4

1. National Institute of Mental Health, "Anxiety Disorders," www.nimh.nih.gov/health/publications/anxiety-disorders/index.shtml?wvsessionid=wv650bd43245ce405884dd789794894544 (accessed April 1, 2014).

2. National Institute of Mental Health, "Anxiety Disorders."

3. Hara Estroff Marano, "The Different Faces of Depression," *Psychology Today*, July–August 2002, reprinted in Jacqueline Langwith, ed., *Perspectives on Diseases and Disorders—Depression* (Farmington Hills, MI: Greenhaven Press, 2009), p. 30.

4. Melvyn Lurie, MD, *Depression: Your Questions Answered* (London: Dorling Kindersley, 2007), p. 63.

5. *Merriam-Webster's Medical Dictionary*, s.v., "bipolar disorder," www2.merriam-webster.com/cgi-bin/mwmedsamp (accessed May 11, 2014).

6. Francis Mark Mondimore, *Depression: The Mood Disease*, rev. ed. (Baltimore and London: Johns Hopkins University Press, 1993).

7. Brian P. Quinn, CSW, PhD, *The Depression Sourcebook*, 2nd ed. (Lincolnwood, IL: Lowell House, 2000), p. 59.

8. Quinn, *The Depression Sourcebook*, p. 59.

9. Quinn, *The Depression Sourcebook*, p. 59.

10. Quinn, *The Depression Sourcebook*, p. 62.

11. Margaret Strock, "Depression Is a Serious Mental Illness," in *Contemporary Issues Companion: Depression*, ed. Emma Carlson Berne (Farmington Hills, MI: Greenhaven Press, 2007), p. 16.

12. Paula Anne Ford-Martin and Teresa G. Odle, "The Causes, Symptoms, and Treatments of Depression," *The Gale Encyclopedia of Medicine*, 3rd ed., Gale, 2007, reprinted in Jacqueline Langwith, ed., *Perspectives on Diseases and Disorders—Depression* (Farmington Hills, MI: Greenhaven Press, 2009), p. 20.

13. Ford-Martin and Odle, "The Causes, Symptoms, and Treatments of Depression," *Gale Encyclopedia*, p. 20

14. Ford-Martin and Odle, "The Causes, Symptoms, and Treatments of Depression," *Gale Encyclopedia*, p. 20.

15. Ford-Martin and Odle, "The Causes, Symptoms, and Treatments of Depression," *Gale Encyclopedia*, p. 20.
16. Kenneth McIntosh, *The History of Depression* (Broomall, PA: Mason Crest Publishers, 2007), p. 27.
17. National Institute of Mental Health (NIMH), "Depression," www.nimh.nih.gov/health/publications/depression/index.shtml (accessed April 1, 2014).
18. NIMH, "Depression."
19. NIMH, "Depression."
20. Lurie, *Depression*, p. 63.
21. Lurie, *Depression*, p. 63.
22. Lurie, *Depression*, p. 63.

a. American Psychiatric Association, *Diagnostic and Statistical Manual of Mental Disorders*, 5th ed. (Arlington, VA: American Psychiatric Association, 2013), p. 189.
b. William F., e-mailed questionnaire, January 19, 2013.
c. Steven, e-mail, March 7, 2014.

Chapter 5

1. Christina, adult reviewing journals from age seventeen, e-mail, March 28, 2014.
2. The National Center on Addiction and Substance Abuse, Columbia University (CASA), "Teen Tipplers: America's Underage Drinking Epidemic," February 2003, www.casacolumbia.org/addiction-research/reports/teen-tipplers-americas-underage-drinking-epidemic (accessed December 17, 2013).
3. CASA, "Teen Tipplers."
4. CASA, "Teen Tipplers."
5. CASA, "Teen Tipplers."
6. Deborah Serani, *Living with Depression: Why Biology and Biography Matter along the Path to Hope and Healing* (Lanham, MD: Rowman & Littlefield, 2011), p. 28.
7. Edward J. Cumella, Martian C. Eberly, and A. David Wall, *Eating Disorders: a Handbook of Christian Treatment* (Nashville, TN: Remuda Ranch, 2008), p. 319.
8. Cumella, Eberly, and Wall, *Eating Disorders*, p. 319.
9. Cumella, Eberly, and Wall, *Eating Disorders*, p. 319.
10. South Carolina Department of Mental Health, "Eating Disorder Statistics, www.state.sc.us/dmh/anorexia/statistics.htm (accessed November 18, 2013).
11. HelpGuide.org, "Cutting & Self-Harm," www.helpguide.org/mental/self_injury.htm (accessed December 17, 2013).
12. HelpGuide.org, "Cutting & Self-Harm."
13. HelpGuide.org, "Cutting & Self-Harm."
14. American Association for Marriage and Family Therapy, "Hair Pulling, Ski Picking and Biting: Body-Focused Repetitive Disorders," in *Mental Health Information for Teens: Health Tips about Mental Wellness and Mental Illness*, ed. Karen Bellenir (Detroit, MI: Omnigraphics, 2010), p. 168.
15. Understanding O.C.Hoarding.D, "Treatment Options for OCHD," understanding_ocd.tripod.com/hoarding2.html (accessed December 17, 2013).

16. Christina, e-mail.

17. Jessica G., "Lois Lee, Founder of a Half-Way House for Underage Prostitutes, Makes Us Believe in Altruism," Jezebel.com, July 7, 2008, jezebel.com/5022638/lois-lee-founder-of-a -half+way-house-for-underge-prostitutes-makes-us-believe-in-altruism (accessed December 17, 2013).

18. Josepha Cheong, MD, Michael Herkov, PhD, and Wayne Goodman, MD, "Depression and Smoking," PsychCentral, psychcentral.com/library/depression_smoking.htm (accessed December 17, 2013).

19. Dr. Daniel Seidman, director of Smoking Cessation Services, Columbia University Medical Center, "Depression, Smoking, and Quitting," *HuffingtonPost: The Blog*, April 20, 2010, www.huffingtonpost.com/daniel-seidman/depression-smoking-and-qu_b_545197.html (accessed December 17, 2013).

20. Centers for Disease Control and Prevention, "History of the Surgeon General's Reports on Smoking and Health," www.cdc.gov/tobacco/data_statistics/sgr/history/ (accessed August 5, 2013).

21. Cheong, Herkov, and Goodman, "Depression and Smoking."

22. Cheong, Herkov and Goodman, "Depression and Smoking."

23. Debra Koenitz, LCPC, ATR-BC, e-mail, June 17, 2013.

24. Mark L. Hatzenbuehler, "The Social Environment and Suicide Attempts in Lesbian, Gay, and Bisexual Youth," *Pediatrics: Journal of the American Academy of Pediatrics*, April 18, 2011, p. 896. pediatrics.aappublications.org/content/early/2011/04/18/peds.2010–3020.abstract (accessed February 7, 2014).

25. Hatzenbuehler, "The Social Environment and Suicide Attempts."

---

a. CASA, "Teen Tipplers."

b. XpurplemacaroniX, "When They Look," *TeenInk.com*, www.teenink.com/hot_topics/ bullying/article/521804/When-They-Look/ (accessed March 29, 2014).

c. National Association of Anorexia Nervosa and Associated Disorders, "Eating Disorders Statistics," www.anad.org/get-information/about-eating-disorders/eating-disorders-statistics/ (accessed December 17, 2013).

d. HelpGuide.org, "Cutting & Self-Harm."

e. Veronica, in-person conversation and questionnaire, June 2013.

f. Understanding O.C.Hoarding.D, "Treatment Options for OCHD."

g. Understanding O.C.Hoarding.D, "Treatment Options for OCHD."

h. Seidman, "Depression, Smoking, and Quitting."

i. Al Desetta, MA, and Sybil Wolin, PhD, eds., *Struggle to Be Strong: True Stories by Teens about Overcoming Tough Times* (Minneapolis, MN: Free Spirit Publishing, Inc., 2000), pp. 134–35.

j. American Medical Association, *Essential Guide to Depression* (New York: Pocket Books, 1998), p. 59.

k. Koenitz, e-mail.

l. Anonymous, adult female looking back at journals from age seventeen, phone interview, June 2012.

m. Charlene Johnson, "My Weight Is No Burden," in Desetta and Wolin, *Struggle to Be Strong*, p. 42.

n. National Institute of Mental Health, "Statistics," www.nimh.nih.gov/health/publications/ suicide-in-the-us-statistics-and-prevention/index.shtml#children (accessed June 26, 2013).

o. R. C. Kessler, G. Borges, and E. E. Walters, "Prevalence of and Risk Factors for Lifetime Suicide Attempts in the National Comorbidity Survey," *Archives of General Psychiatry* 56, no. 7 (1999): pp. 617–26.

p. Centers for Disease Control and Prevention, National Center for Injury Prevention and Control, Web-Based Injury statistics Query and Reporting System (WISQARS): www.cdc.gov/ncipc/wisqars (accessed June 26, 2013).

q. Centers for Disease Control and Prevention, WISQARS.

r. Centers for Disease Control and Prevention, WISQARS.

s. Veronica, in-person conversation and questionnaire.

Chapter 6

1. Melvyn Lurie, MD, *Depression: Your Questions Answered* (New York: Dorling Kindersley, 2007), p. 114.
2. Lurie, *Depression*, p. 114.
3. Lurie, *Depression*, p. 115.
4. Susan, questionnaire e-mailed April 28, 2013.
5. Lydia Bjornlund, *Depression* (Farmington Hills, MI: Lucent Books, 2010), p. 66.
6. Lurie, *Depression*, p. 115.
7. Bev Cobain, RN, C, *When Nothings Matters Anymore: A Survival Guide for Depressed Teens*, rev. and updated ed. (Minneapolis, MN: Free Spirit Publishing, 2007), p. 13.
8. Cait Irwin, *Monochrome Days: A Firsthand Account of One Teenager's Experience with Depression* (New York: Oxford University Press, 2007), p. 78.
9. Irwin, *Monochrome Days*, p. 16.
10. Bjornlund, *Depression*, p. 66.
11. Bjornlund, *Depression*, p. 66.
12. Christopher A. Bogle, "Learning to Forgive," in *Struggle to Be Strong: True Stories by Teens about Overcoming Tough Times*, ed. Al Desetta, MA, and Sybil Wolin, PhD, (Minneapolis, MN: Free Spirit Publishing, 2000), p. 81.
13. Bogle, "Learning to Forgive," p. 83.
14. Bogle, "Learning to Forgive," p. 81.
15. Frederic Flach, MD, KHS, *The Secret Strength of Depression*, 3rd ed. (New York: Hatherleigh Press, 2002), p. 95.
16. Flach, *The Secret Strength of Depression*, p. 99.
17. Flach, *The Secret Strength of Depression*, p. 99.
18. Flach, *The Secret Strength of Depression*, p. 100.
19. Bjornlund, *Depression*, p. 65–66.
20. Bjornlund, *Depression*, p. 66.

a. CGS, questionnaire, May 2012.
b. Bjornlund, *Depression*, p. 65.
c. Lurie, *Depression*, pp. 158–59.
d. U.S. Equal Employment Opportunity Commission, "Facts about the Americans with Disabilities Act," www.eeoc.gov/facts/fs-ada.html (accessed June 17, 2013).

Chapter 7

1. Stanford School of Medicine, "Major Depression and Genetics," depressiongenetics.stanford.edu/mddandgenes.html (accessed December 20, 2013).
2. Wendy Boswell, "Luke Wilson in Tears over Brother Owen's Suicide Attempt, Crushable, August 30, 2007, www.crushable.com/2007/08/30/entertainment/luke-wilson-in-tears-over-brother-owens-attempted-suicide/ (accessed May 23, 2013).
3. Karen S. Schneider, with Bob Meadows, "Owen Wilson: What Happened?" *People* (September 10, 2007), www.people.com/people/archive/article/0,,20060242,00.html (accessed June 19, 2013).
4. Boswell, "Luke Wilson in Tears."
5. Anne Courtright, *Reaching Your Goals: The Ultimate Teen Guide* (Lanham, MD: Scarecrow Press, 2009), p. 22.

a. Literature_Darling, "Sister," *TeenInk.com*, www.teenink.com/hot_topics/what_matters/article/547227/Sister/ (accessed March 29, 2014).
b. Jake, phone conversation, March 27, 2014.
c. Jamie A. Seba, *Gays and Mental Health: Fighting Depression, Saying No to Suicide* (Broomall, PA: Mason Crest Publishers, 2011), pp. 26–27.

Chapter 8

1. Ann Van Den Bogaert, PhD; Kristel Sleegers, MD, PhD; Sonia De Zutter; Lien Heyrman; Karl-Fredrik Norrback, MD, PhD; Rolf Adolfsson, MD, PhD; Christine Van Broeckhoven, PhD, DSc; and Jurgen Del-Favero Jr., PhD, "Association of Brain-Specific Tryptophan Hydroxylase, TPH2, with Unipolar and Bipolar Disorder in a Northern Swedish, Isolated Population," *Archives of General Psychiatry* 63, no. 10 (October 2006):1103–10. doi:10.1001/archpsyc.63.10.1103. Depression Facts, "Is Depression Hereditary?" www.aboutdepressionfacts.com/is-depression-hereditary.html (accessed March 25, 2013).
2. Van Den Bogaert et al., "Association of Brain-Specific Tryptophan Hydroxylase," 1103–10; Depression Facts, "Is Depression Hereditary?"
3. Liz Szabo, "Committing a Mentally Ill Adult Is Complex," *USA Today*, January 13, 2013, www.usatoday.com/story/news/nation/2013/01/07/mental-illiness-civil-commitment/1814301/ (accessed December 19, 2013).
4. Szabo, "Committing a Mentally Ill Adult Is Complex."

a. Hazelden, "What Is an Intervention?" www.hazelden.org/web/public/faqintervention.page (accessed March 25, 2013).
b. William, questionnaire, e-mailed in 2012.
c. Hannah, conversation, June 2012.
d. William, phone conversation, April 2012.
e. William, phone conversation.

Chapter 9

1. Janine Boldrin. "How Are the Kids? After More Than a Decade of War, the Children of Reservists Feel the Strain of Deployment," *Officer*, May–June 2013, pp. 17–18.
2. Boldrin, "How Are the Kids?" pp. 17–18
3. Boldrin, "How Are the Kids?" p. 17.
4. Erin, e-mail, October 2013.
5. Erin, e-mail.
6. Erin, e-mail.
7. Valerie Jarrett, "Ending Bullying in Our Schools and Communities," *President Obama and the LGBT Community* (blog), April 20, 2012, www.whitehouse.gov/blog/2012/04/20/ending-bullying-our-schools-communities (accessed January 19, 2013).
8. Cited in Tori DeAngelis, "New Data on Lesbian, Gay, and Bisexual Mental Health," *Monitor on Psychology* 33, no. 2 (February 2002), www.apa.org/monitor/feb02/newdata.aspx (accessed September 19, 2013).
9. DeAngelis, "New Data."
10. T. DeAngelis, "Parents' Rejection of a Child's Sexual Orientation Fuels Mental Health Problems," *Monitor on Psychology* 40, no. 3 (2009), www.apa.org/monitor/2009/03/orientation.aspx (accessed January 23, 2014). Article cites information from Caitlyn Ryan, PhD, of San Francisco University originally published in *Pediatrics* 123, no. 1 (January 2009).
11. Quoted in Laurel G. Morales, "For Native Americans, Mental Health Budget Cuts Hit Hard," National Public Radio, September 12, 2013, www.npr.org/blogs/codeswitch/2013/09/12/221408312/for-native-americans-mental-health-budget-cuts-hit-hard (accessed January 23, 2014).
12. Morales, "For Native Americans."
13. PewResearch, "Summary of Key Findings," Religion and Public Life Project, religions.pewforum.org/reports (accessed October 1, 2013).
14. Engy Abdelkader, "Bullying Targets 'the Other,'" *Record* (New Jersey newspaper) and Arab American Forum, November 28, 2010, www.aafusa.org/bullying.aspx (accessed October 1, 2013).
15. Abdelkader, "Bullying Targets 'the Other.'"
16. Abdelkader, "Bullying Targets 'the Other.'"

---

a. Dennis K. Orthner and Roderick Rose, *Survey Report: Adjustment of Army Children to Deployment Separations* (Chapel Hill: University of North Carolina at Chapel Hill). National Alliance on Mental Illness (NAMI) 2010, 2nd Edition, reference book for families.
b. Jerilyn Marler, *Lily Hates Goodbyes* (Beaverton, OR: Quincy Companion Books, 2011).
c. Erin, e-mail.
d. Victoria Stuart-Cassel, Ariana Bell, and J. Fred Springer, *Analysis of State Bullying Laws and Policies* (Folsom, CA: EMT Associates, 2011), cited in Mathangi Subramanian, EdD, *Bullying: The Ultimate Teen Guide* (Lanham, MD: Rowman & Littlefield, forthcoming).
e. Phone conversation with Deb, gay adult, Summer 2012.
f. NAMI, American Indian Alaska Native statistic sheets, 2010.
g. National Institute of Mental Health, "Suicide in America: Frequently Asked Questions," www.nimh.nih.gov/health/publications/suicide-in-america/index.shtml (accessed September 19, 2013).

Chapter 10

1. Melody Beattie, *Codependent No More: How to Stop Controlling Others and Start Caring for Yourself*, 2nd rev. ed., (Center City, MN: Hazelden, 2009).

a. William, e-mail, March 29, 2014.
b. CGS, phone conversation, June 2012.
c. Laurie Halse Anderson, *Wintergirls* (New York: Viking, 2009).
d. William, phone conversation, June 2012.

Chapter 11

1. Bev Cobain, RN, C, *When Nothing Matters Anymore: A Survival Guide for Depressed Teens* (Minneapolis, MN: Free Spirit Publishing, 2007), pp. 32–33.
2. Judy Monroe Peterson, *Frequently Asked Questions about Antidepressants* (New York: Rosen Publishing Group, 2010), pp. 31–32.
3. Peterson, *Frequently Asked Questions*, p. 32.
4. Peterson, *Frequently Asked Questions*, p. 32.
5. Peterson, *Frequently Asked Questions*, p. 32.
6. Peterson, *Frequently Asked Questions*, p. 32.
7. Cait Irwin, *Monochrome Days* (New York: Oxford University Press, 2007), pp. 81–82.
8. Maureen Empfield, MD, and Nicholas Bakalar, *Understanding Teenage Depression* (New York: Henry Holt, 2001), p. 167.
9. Greg Mone, "Deep Brain Stimulation Is a Promising New Treatment for Depression," in *Perspectives on Diseases and Disorders—Depression*, ed. Jacqueline Langwith (Farmington Hills, MI: Greenhaven Press, 2008), p. 50.
10. Empfield and Bakalar, *Understanding Teenage Depression*, p. 167.
11. Empfield and Bakalar, *Understanding Teenage Depression*, p. 154.
12. U.S. Dept. of Health and Human Services and U.S. Dept. of Agriculture, "Dietary Guidelines for Americans—2005," www.nlm.nih.gov/medlineplus/ency/article/002332.htm (accessed December 30, 2013).
13. Dr. Purvi Vyas, PharmD, in-person interview at Osco in Grayslake, Illinois, October 7, 2013.
14. Peterson, *Frequently Asked Questions*, p. 38.
15. Center for Women's Mental Health at Massachusetts General Hospital, "PMS and Premenstrual Dysphoric Disorder," in *Mental Health Information for Teens: Health Tips about Mental Wellness and Mental Illness*, 3rd ed., ed. Karen Bellenir (Detroit, MI: Omnigraphics, 2010), p. 99.
16. Pam Belluck, "Promising Depression Therapy," *New York Times*, February 12, 2013, p. D6.
17. Belluck, "Promising Depression Therapy," p. D6.
18. Deborah Serani, *Living with Depression: Why Biology and Biography Matter along the Path to Home and Healing* (Lanham, MD: Rowman & Littlefield, 2011), p. 38.
19. Raymond Crowe, MD, professor in the Department of Psychiatry at the University of Iowa College of Medicine; quoted in Bellenir, *Mental Health Information*, p. 267.
20. MedlinePlus, "Electroconvulsive Therapy," www.nlm.nih.gov/medlineplus/ency/article/007474.htm (accessed August 21, 2013).

21. MedlinePlus, "Electroconvulsive Therapy."

22. Denise Minger, "The Negative Health Effects of Drinking Coffee," www.livestrong.com/article/128501-negative-health-effects-drinking -coffee/ (accessed June 1, 2014).

23. Dr. Purvi Vyas, in-person interview.

24. Courtney from Parenting Teens (1-866-395-7599), phone call, February 25, 2014.

a. Kathryn, e-mail, July 2013.

b. Susan, questionnaire, summer 2012.

c. Deb, phone call, April 2013.

d. Tamara Ballard, "Walking Out the Anger," in *The Struggle to Be Strong: True Stories by Teens about Overcoming Tough Times*, ed. Al Desetta, MA, and Sybil Wolin, PhD (Minneapolis, MN: Free Spirit Publishing, 2000), p. 121.

e. Transcribed from Al-Anon Family Groups, "Members and Professionals Talk about Alateen," www.al-anon.org/members-and-professionals-talk-about-alateen (accessed March 29, 2014).

f. Empfield and Bakalar, *Understanding Teenage Depression*, p. 161.

g. National Alliance on Mental Illness, *A Family Guide: What Families Need to Know about Adolescent Depression* (Arlington, VA: NAMI, 2010), www.nami.org/Content/ContentGroups/CAAC/FamilyGuidePRINT.pdf (accessed January 19, 2014).

h. Veronica, questionnaire, summer 2013.

i. Dr. James Fugedy, phone call verifying quotes about tDCS on website www.transcranialbrainstimulation.com, May 2013.

j. Fugedy, phone call.

Chapter 12

1. Susan, e-mail, April 28, 2013.

2. Seth, e-mail, April 29, 2013.

3. Bella, phone interview, April 30, 2013.

4. Kathryn, e-mail, September 25, 2013.

5. Sarah Glynn, "Creativity Closely Linked To Mental Illness," *Medical News Today*, October 17, 2012, www.medicalnewstoday.com/articles/251568.php (accessed January 3, 2014).

6. Merely Me, "7 Presidents Who Battled Depression," HealthCentral, February 20, 2012, www.healthcentral.com/depression/c/84292/150467/7-depression/ (accessed March 10, 2014).

a. Nancy Schimelpfening, "Jim Carrey," www.depression.about.com/od/famous/p/jimcarrey.htm (accessed June 1, 2014).

b. MetrazolElectricity, "Jim Carey on Spirituality and Overcoming Depression" YouTube video, www.youtube.com/watch?v=KfWN5EW5eo4 (accessed January 3, 2014).

c. Deborah Serani, *Living with Depression: Why Biology and Biography Matter along the Path to Hope and Healing* (Lanham, MD: Rowman & Littlefield, 2011), pp. 115–27.

Resources

Reference Books about Depression

Berlinger, Norman. *Rescuing Your Teenager from Depression* (New York: Harper-Collins, 2005).

Bjornlund, Lydia. *Depression* (New York: HarperCollins, 2005).

Canfield, Jack, Mark Victor Hansen, Stephanie H. Meyer, and John Meyer, comps. *Chicken Soup for the Teen Soul: Real-Life Stories by Real Teens* (New York: Scholastic, 2007).

Cobain, Bev. *When Nothing Matters Anymore: A Survival Guide for Depressed Teens* (Minneapolis, MN: Free Spirit Publishing, 1998).

DePaulo, Jr., J. Raymond. *Understanding Depression: What We Know & What You Can Do About It* (New York: John Wiley & Sons, 2002).

Desetta, Al, and Sybil Wolin, eds. *Struggle to Be Strong: True Stories by Teens about Overcoming Tough Times* (Minneapolis, MN: Free Spirit Publishing, 2000).

Empfield, Maureen, and Nicholas Bakalar. *Understanding Teenage Depression: A Guide to Diagnosis, Treatment, and Management* (New York: Henry Holt, 2001).

Evans, Dwight L., and Linda Wasmar Andrews. *If Your Adolescent Has Depression or Bipolar Disorder* (New York: Oxford University Press, 2005).

Fitzgerald, Helen. *The Grieving Teen: A Guide for Teenagers and Their Friends* (New York: Fireside, 2000).

Fitzpatrick, Carol, and John Sharry. *Coping with Depression in Young People: A Guide for Parents* (West Sussex, England: John Wiley & Sons, 2004).

Ilardi, Stephen S. *The Depression CURE: The 6-Step Program to Beat Depression without Drugs* (Cambridge, MA: Da Capo Press, 2009).

Irwin, Cait. *Monochrome Days: A Firsthand Account of One Teenager's Experience with Depression* (New York: Oxford University Press, 2007).

Kübler-Ross, Elisabeth. *On Grief and Grieving: Finding the Meaning of Grief through the Five Stages of Loss* (New York: Scribner, 2005).

Lurie, Melvyn. *Depression: Your Questions Answered* (New York: DK Publishing, 2007).

Machoian, Lisa. *The Disappearing Girl: Learning the Language of Teenage Depression* (New York: Penguin Publishing Group, 2006).

Martin, Michael J. *Teen Depression* (Farmington Hills, MI: Thomas Gale, 2005).

Miller, Allen R. *Teen's Guides: Living with Depression* (New York: Facts on File, 2008).

Noonan, Susan J. *Managing Your Depression: What You Can Do to Feel Better* (Baltimore, MD: Johns Hopkins University Press, 2013).

Peterson, Judy Monroe. *Frequently Asked Questions about Antidepressants* (New York: Rosen Publishing Group, 2010).

Runyon, Brent. *The Burn Journals* (New York: Vintage Books, 2004).

Seba, Jamie A. *Gays and Mental Health: Fighting Depression, Saying No to Suicide* (Bromall, PA: Mason Crest Publishers, 2011).

Organizations

American Academy of Child and Adolescent Psychiatry (AACAP)
www.aacap.org/AACAP/Families_and_Youth/Resource_Centers/Depression_Resource_Center/Home.aspx
3615 Wisconsin Avenue NW
Washington, DC 20016-3007
Phone: 202-966-7300

American Psychological Association (APA)
www.apa.org
750 First Street NE
Washington, DC 20002-4242
Phone: 202-336-5500
Toll Free: 800-374-2721

American Society for Adolescent Psychiatry (ASAP)
www.adolpsych.org
PO Box 570218
Dallas, TX 75357-0218
Phone: 972-613-0985

Depression and Bipolar Support Alliance (DBSA)
www.dbsalliance.org
730 N. Franklin Street, Suite 501
Chicago, IL 60654-7225
Phone: 800-826-3632

The International Foundation for Research and Education on Depression (iFred)
www.ifred.org

PO Box 17598
Baltimore, MD 21297-1598
E-mail: info@ifred.org

Mayo Clinic
www.mayoclinic.com
200 First Street SW
Rochester, MN 55905
Phone: 507-284-2511

Mental Health America
www.mentalhealthamerica.net
2000 N. Beauregard Street, 6th Floor
Alexandria, VA 22311
Phone: 703-684-7722
Toll free: 800-969-6642

National Alliance on Mental Health (NAMI)
www.nami.org
3803 N. Fairfax Drive, Suite 100
Arlington, VA 22203
Phone: 703-524-7600
Helpline: 800-950-6264

National Institute of Mental Health (NIMH)
www.nimh.nih.gov
6001 Executive Blvd.
Bethesda, MD 20892
Phone: 301-443-4513
Toll Free: 866-615-6464
E-mail: nimhinfo@nih.gov

National Suicide Prevention Lifeline
www.suicidepreventionlifeline.org
Toll Free: 800-273-TALK (8255)

Helpful Website on Depression

www.therainbowbabies.com/Depression.html

Index

About the Author

Tina P. Schwartz is a writer from the suburbs of Chicago. She graduated from Columbia College, Chicago, with a BA in marketing communication, advertising emphasis. She enjoys writing, watching movies, and spending time with her family and friends. After many years, she gave up a career in advertising to open her own literary agency, The Purcell Agency, LLC, in 2012. Schwartz is the author of *Organ Transplants: A Survival Guide for the Entire Family: The Ultimate Teen Guide* (2005) and *Writing and Publishing: The Ultimate Teen Guide* (2010), both published by Scarecrow Press.

Tina likes to meet many people while doing speaking engagements, attending conferences, doing author visits, and attending book signings. If you'd like to learn more go to www.thepurcellagency.com or www.tinapschwartz.com.